Phil Redmond's

THE OFFICIAL COMPANION

Phil Redmond's

HOLLYOAKS

A MERSEY TELEVISION COMPANY

THE OFFICIAL COMPANION

Matthew Evans

First published 2002 by Channel 4 Books
an imprint of Pan Macmillan Ltd
Pan Macmillan, 20 New Wharf Road, London N1 9RR
Basingstoke and Oxford
Associated companies throughout the world
www.panmacmillan.com

ISBN 0 7522 2000 4

1 3 5 7 9 8 6 4 2

A CIP catalogue record for this book is available from the British Library.

Photographs © Hollyoaks Productions Limited 2002

Designed by seagulls

Printed and bound by Mackays of Chatham Ltd, Chatham, Kent

This book accompanies the television series *Hollyoaks*
made by Hollyoaks Productions Limited for Channel 4.

Executive Producer: Phil Redmond
Series Producer: Jo Hallows

CONTENTS

As soon as *Grange Hill* became a staple diet for school children across Britain, the audience constantly asked me to develop a show that revealed what happened to the older characters when they left school. A programme aimed entirely at the teenage audience.

However, any plans for such a show were put on the back burner while I developed *Brookside* for Channel 4 which, unsurprisingly, took up the majority of my time. Still, the idea of a teenage drama was one I intended to come back to.

It was not until 1995 that I came back to it, when Channel 4 appealed for independent television companies to make proposals for a teenage drama. I decided that it would be the perfect opportunity to make the show I'd wanted to make for over a decade and so pitched an idea that was simply called *The Teen Soap.*

As with *Grange Hill* I was fortunate enough to be in the right place, at the right time, with the right idea. It couldn't have come at a better time; whilst the schedules were brimming with export shows such as *Beverley Hills 90210, Neighbours* and *Home and Away*, there was no British counterpart and there was clearly a huge demand for such a show. The submission was successful and within months, production had commenced.

The premise of the show was that it would be set around the lives of seven teenagers in Chester and would look at their lives in an irreverent and light-hearted fashion. It was quite simply about the two biggest issues in life: Who am I and where am I going? It was also about going out, enjoying yourself, listening to music, and getting on and off with the opposite sex.

On 23 October 1995, 3 million homes across the UK were introduced to Kurt, Jambo, Tony, Louise, Maddie, Natasha and Dawn for the very first time. At first, it was transmitted once a week and as a new show, *Hollyoaks* attracted some considerable press attention. Inevitably, the critics were quick to, well, live up to their job description and criticize. The intended audience got it though and in July 1996, having realized that they had a hit on their hands, Channel 4 commissioned *Hollyoaks* to become a twice-weekly soap.

In a genre of television where so many have failed, why then has *Hollyoaks* remained so successful? Undoubtedly one of the strengths of the show is that it has preserved the ingredients that made it so distinctive when it first began: its irreverence and its sense of humour.

I did inject issues into the show, but only at the request of the audience. They wanted to see a British teenage soap dealing with British social issues. Indeed, episodes such as the death of Natasha can now be seen as significant turning points. Despite heavier issues finding their way into the show, *Hollyoaks* has never lost its sense of humour and will always regard the comedy as equally as important as the drama. Laughter is often entangled with tragedy and *Hollyoaks* has never lost sight of this.

Creating characters is never an easy task in developing a new show, especially with such a demanding audience; yet looking back, there is no question of the huge impact achieved by the likes of Kurt and Jambo. Whilst the majority of these older faces have moved on, they have left an indelible print on the show and have remained a benchmark for later characters to leap from. Of course, as old faces leave, new faces arrive and while Kurt and Jambo were fronting the show back in 1995, the likes of Geri and Luke moved it into the twenty-first century.

The show began with a tentative once-a-week slot – it is now shown four times a week on Channel 4 with an average audience of over 4 million. It is broadcast all around the world and has spawned its own spin-off series; it has been nominated for a BAFTA three out of a possible four years; it has triumphed at the British Soap Awards and has produced such seminal episodes as the one depicting Luke's rape.

The success of *Hollyoaks* is testament to the power of an audience – whatever the critics say – it is always the audience who has the casting vote. *Hollyoaks: The Official Companion* is a tribute to their loyalty and support.

Phil Redmond, April 2002

Ever since it first appeared on our screens in October 1995, fans have taken *Hollyoaks* to their hearts. Now, for the first time, this book chronicles the past and present of this unique soap. From Kurt Benson's very first screen appearance, through to Ellie's dramatic return, *Hollyoaks* has entertained us with scores of unforgettable stories and characters on its seven-year journey.

And what eventful years they've been! Remember when the very first *Hollyoaks* babe, Natasha, died on the dancefloor after Rob spiked her drink? Or Lucy, Tony, Ruth and Lewis's dramatic escape after Rob trapped them in the watertank? Remember the day that Julie jilted Tony at the altar? Remember the boys in Ibiza, enjoying a short-lived period of innocence before their lives were turned upside down…?

Yes? Then relive those classic moments at leisure with *Hollyoaks: The Official Companion… No?* Get reading!

Once you've revelled in those classic moments, take a walk down memory lane as we look at the lives of some of those much-loved characters. Everyone has a favourite *Hollyoaks* character, be it Jambo, Geri, Kurt or Luke. This book celebrates the highs and lows of all of these people, from the show's very first villain, Rob Hawthorne, through to the cult figure that is Mr C. Relive the terrible moments of Luke's rape; the tragic moment Jambo lost his beloved Dawn, as well as the comic escapades of Max and O.B and the assortment of irreverent characters that have passed through Chester over the years.

This official companion also features a whole host of stories and anecdotes about the show including many little-known facts that you can use to beguile your friends. For example – did you know that one of the original suggestions for a title for the show was *Today Not Tomorrow*? Series creator Phil Redmond eventually opted for *Hollyoaks,* as he felt it sounded like a respectable suburb that would be recognizable in any city.

Hollyoaks prides itself on being different from its competitors, using what can only be described as the *Hollyoaks* 'spin' on life. For instance, no other show could combine the high drama of Luke's trial with a naturist party and get away with it. The funeral of Jill Osborne saw the vicar knocked out by the coffin and the brutal moments of Luke's rape were juxtaposed with Max's first sexual experience with Chloe. It is now taken for granted that life for the residents of Hollyoaks Village will never run smoothly; yet it can be guaranteed that there will be plenty of laughter along the way.

Sit back and enjoy, as we begin the story of seven friends who live in a small suburb in Chester, who could never have predicted how intriguing their lives would become to millions of teenagers around the world…

KURT BENSON *Played by Jeremy Edwards*

Kurt had two passions in life – his motorbike and his music. And he was intent on achieving just two things – becoming a rock star and getting his hands on the desirable Natasha! Kurt had been best friends with Tony since primary school, but often despaired at his submissive nature. Kurt was the eldest of three children, his younger brother Ollie being the constant bane of his life.

JAMES 'JAMBO' BOLTON *Played by Will Mellor*

Jambo was originally a friend of Kurt's, but soon became friends with the rest of the gang. Jambo had an idiosyncratic approach to life – he disliked convention and had a naturally inquisitive mind, often pondering on life's little mysteries, such as the theory of tumbling toast!

TONY HUTCHINSON *Played by Nick Pickard*

Tony was an assistant chef at Riverbank College and was Kurt's oldest friend. Tony was a loveable geek and the sort of guy who would instantly and completely fall in love. The antithesis of Kurt, sensitive and keen to settle down, Tony lacked Kurt's confidence with women, but was soon to meet Julie and fall head over heels in love.

NATASHA ANDERSON *Played by Shebah Ronay*

Sophisticated, glamorous and feisty – Natasha was the ultimate object of Kurt's desire. Natasha was friends

Dawn

Tony

Jambo

Natasha

with Maddie, Dawn and Louise, and spent much of her time trying to fend off Kurt's advances.

DAWN CUNNINGHAM *Played by Lisa Williamson*

Spirited, independent and friendly to everyone, Dawn was Natasha's best friend. She worked in Maddie's mother's interior design shop. Dawn had continual problems with her mother's boyfriend, Terry, but refused to let anything get her down. With their tumultuous love lives, her friends could always rely on Dawn for a shoulder to cry on.

LOUISE TAYLOR *Played by Brett O'Brien*

Earth mother Louise was friends with Natasha, Dawn and Maddie. Louise was a hopeless romantic, causing her friends no end of trouble in her pursuit of the 'perfect' man. Louise was also obsessed with anything supernatural and lived her life according to what her horoscope dictated.

MADDIE PARKER *Played by Yasmin Bannerman*

Maddie was the streetwise and sassy siren who ran Parkers restaurant. She was good friends with Natasha, Louise and Dawn. Despite a brief dalliance with Kurt, Maddie was young, free and single, and always on the lookout for a man.

Kurt

Maddie

Louise

WRITTEN BY Phil Redmond
DIRECTED BY Ken Horn

On 23 October 1995, 2.9 million homes tuned in to watch the much-hyped and much-talked about new teen drama *Hollyoaks*. They'd seen the bill-boards, read the multiple articles and spreads and finally the moment was here. People had high expectations and suddenly the now familiar music began playing for the very first time...

Episode 1 Sc. 1 **Woodland** (Day) 3.30pm

We open on a very rural vista – on the edge of a wood with over-grown bushes, small trees and long grass. Very idyllic until...

In the distance a deep mechanical roar is heard. After a moment the foliage starts to part, as something rushes through the under-growth...

Suddenly a car bursts out. We see that this is obviously someone's pride and joy. It has had a lot of hours of sweat and blood lavished on it to turn what was once an old MKII Ford Consul into a very sinister-looking, matt-grey Saturday-night cruiser, complete with airbrushed artwork along each side – flames from the front wheels and a 'flying virgin' on the bonnet...

The car slides to a halt in a hail of gravel and dead foliage. Its engine and exhaust are pumping out raw power, but, unfortunately, it also appears to be pumping out smoke from under the bonnet...

If viewers had been expecting to make sense of what was going on from the very first scene, they would have been thrown. Instead, they were presented with a series of scenes that encapsulated the lives of the teenagers in Chester. The very first scene showed a car hurtling through wasteground, yet before there was even a chance to see who was driving, the scene cut to a cluttered bedroom containing a bizarre collection of memorabilia, ranging from road signs to music and car posters. By the window a computer was printing off what looked like a party invitation. Suddenly a figure walked into frame, collected his invitations, expressed his delight and walked out of the room. Of course, by now we know that this was Kurt, but the viewer of the first episode had yet to piece all the fragments together. What followed was a montage of glimpses into the lives of the residents of Hollyoaks, without any dialogue whatsoever. The scene cut back to the car on the wasteground as four teenagers scrambled out. Just as they managed to get away from the car, it exploded into a ball of flames.

Next we met – albeit briefly – Dawn as she got into a driving school car, Natasha, who was waiting at the gates of Riverbank College and Kurt on his Yamaha DT125. We cut backwards and forwards between these characters, still without dialogue, as Dawn arrived home to be met by her mother running

DIRECTOR KEN HORN ON THE SHOOT OF THIS EPISODE

'The whole epic sequence without dialogue took over a week to shoot. We did some hitherto never-done motorcycle stunts, like doing wheelies and going through gates and doing doughnuts. Luckily we had a terrific stunt driver. Jeremy wasn't riding the bike, so we had to do a wide shot with the stunt driver and then Jeremy would do the single shot – though he hated that because he wanted to do the stunts! We also had the explosion; we had two cars – a real one and fake one, but only one set of wheels! It took about one and a half hours to change the wheels over!

'I remember that Kurt and Jambo were only cast a few days before we started shooting. Jeremy Edwards hadn't acted before, so it was a real baptism of fire for him, but he was terrific.'

down the path, carrying a milk bottle, which she then threw at the driving school car and then back to Natasha on a bus and what appeared to be Kurt driving alongside, evidently looking to see if she was on board. Then we saw Kurt's pursuit of Natasha curtailed when he was spotted by a police car that performed a hasty three-point turn and went after him in hot pursuit. With a series of clever manoeuvres, he managed to shake them off.

This was all designed to intrigue the audience and provoke them into piecing the action and characters together. By the time Kurt uttered his first line when he arrived at the college canteen to see Tony, viewers were already desperate to know the consequences of the crash; what the party invitations were for; why Dawn's mother had reacted so violently and what *was* going on between Kurt and Natasha? We soon got the answers we needed. Kurt's kid brother Ollie was exposed as the 'thief' who had stolen Kurt's car; the invitations were for Louise's party – which, coincidentally, Kurt and his friends had been banned from attending. And finally, we found out that Natasha's younger sister had been a passenger in the car with Ollie, provoking a confrontation in the hospital between Natasha and Kurt.

If that wasn't enough, we met Jambo as he made what was evidently his trademark entrance climbing through Kurt's bedroom window. As the boys managed to blag their way into Louise's party, the traumas continued when Louise discovered her boyfriend with another girl, prompting Kurt to intervene, defending Louise's honour by punching her now ex-boyfriend

> **DID YOU KNOW...?**
>
> The final scene where Kurt and the Alsatian stood face to face was in fact two separate shots joined together in post-production.

Joe. This noble deed earned Kurt the honour of escorting the beguiling Natasha home to The Dog in the Pond where her father was landlord. Just when Kurt thought he was on to a good thing, his chances were scuppered when Natasha told him that there was no way he was getting a kiss. Kurt walked away, uttering the fateful line, 'Guess this isn't one of my better days'. However, refusing to take 'no' for an answer, he went back to Natasha's door, only to be met by her father, Greg and his two Alsatians, one of which leapt towards Kurt...

First episodes are notoriously difficult to get right, but this one left the audience with enough of a taste for the lives of Kurt and his friends to want to tune into episode two and discover whether Louise had got over Joe and whether Kurt would finally get his hands on Natasha. Some critics remarked on its lack of issues, yet *Hollyoaks* was keen to show that not every teenager's life was burdened with problems. As the show developed, tragedy and heartache would inevitably follow. But after this first tantalizing peep at the seven friends in Chester, there wasn't a teenage boy among the 2.9 million viewers who didn't want to be Kurt and there wasn't a girl who wouldn't have given her right arm to be Natasha. One thing was certain – these characters would be sticking around for quite some time.

The Bensons

OCTOBER 1995

Following the car explosion in episode one, Kurt continues to chase Ollie for the money to pay for his car, whilst playing cat and mouse with the police. Louise struggles to come to terms with splitting up with Joe and Dawn spends most of her time hiding from her mother's creepy boyfriend, Terry. Meanwhile, ice maiden Natasha tries her best to fend off Kurt's advances and finally Tony meets Julie and it's love at first sight.

NOVEMBER 1995

Kurt tries to help Louise get over Joe and sets up a Ouija board, planning to 'fix' it so that the 'other side' would tell her to forget about him. The plan backfires when, thanks to Jambo, Louise is led to believe that Kurt should be the next object of her affection. Meanwhile, Jambo's object of affection is Margaret the cow, whom he insists on taking wherever he goes. Kurt throws a party and gets heavy with Louise until she breaks up with him – much to his relief! Tony enlists Dawn's help when he worries he might have lost his job after sneaking out to see Julie, and wide boy Lewis organizes a computer competition at the college and uses Tony as his secret weapon.

DECEMBER 1995

The gang head off to Alton Towers, but are sidetracked when they hear a mysterious broadcast on Bazz's pirate radio – was there a UFO in the woods? The gang investigate but, instead of little green men, they are met by the police! The boys finally arrive but yet again, Kurt misses out on getting his hands on Natasha. Jambo is the subject of gossip when he is spotted with a mysterious woman, but Tony and Kurt are disappointed to learn that she's his mother! Christmas is looming and Kurt is left with the dilemma of choosing between a family Christmas and spending it with Natasha. Natasha wins but

Christmas in The Dog in the Pond.

she loses interest when she sees Kurt bonding with her father. And will Kurt ever locate the 'Unidentified Bleeping Object' that wakes him up every morning?

JANUARY 1996

The year begins with a party at the Bensons'. Kurt is disappointed to learn that Natasha's gone away but soon cheers up when he meets her cousin, Ruth Osborne. Dawn urges her mother not to marry Terry, but will she listen? Maddie beats Tony at a computer game contest and Tony later chastizes himself for accepting a lift home from her – does this mean he's been unfaithful to Julie? Kurt finally gets to go on a date with Ruth – but what about Natasha?

FEBRUARY 1996

Dawn encourages Jambo on a mission to track down his father, while Ruth worries about deceiving Natasha by seeing Kurt. Meanwhile, everyone in *Hollyoaks* gets a mystery Valentine's card and speculation is rife until Ollie confesses that he was the mystery sender. Louise sets her sights on Dermot, the handsome guy who has offered to help her organize the college revue, and Maddie is worried when she gets a creepy card. Ollie finally confesses to Kurt that he is behind the 'Unidentified Bleeping Object'. Jambo and Kurt are persuaded to take part in Louise's pancake race and Kurt is annoyed when Ruth teams up with his old enemy, Rob Hawthorne.

MARCH 1996

Louise organizes a fortune-telling night at The Dog and Tony worries that she might predict doom for his relationship with Julie. Meanwhile, Maddie begins to worry that someone is following her. Elsewhere, Rob sets his sights on Lucy Benson and Dermot turns his attentions to Natasha. Lucy turns eighteen and makes sure her birthday party is a night to remember! Tragedy occurs when Natasha collapses and dies. Hollyoaks mourns her death and the finger of suspicion soon points to Rob and Dermot. Dawn is so distressed that she confesses to Jambo that at sixteen she had a daughter who she gave up for adoption. After learning of Natasha's death, Dawn's sister Jude returns to Chester.

APRIL 1996

Dawn discovers the address of Jambo's father. Rob is consumed with guilt over Natasha's death and breaks up with Lucy. Meanwhile, Jude and Dawn confront their mother about Terry's inappropriate behaviour, but Angela refuses to listen. Rob eventually unburdens himself to Lucy. Tony announces his engagement to Julie, and Kurt and Bazz organize a seance, hoping to get Rob to confess about his role in Natasha's death. Ollie meets the mysterious Susi, who has moved into the flat above the video shop. Louise reveals that Natasha has 'visited' her and told her that she was murdered. Meanwhile, Jambo tries to find Dawn's daughter.

NATASHA'S DEATH

Written by Roy Boulter
Directed by Jo Hallows
Broadcast 11 March 1996

Since its debut in October 1995, *Hollyoaks* had attracted some criticism for its seeming reluctance to deal with heavy issues, and had been labelled by some critics as 'the soft soap' and 'the soap without issues'. In answer to these critics and in a determined effort to portray the lives of teenagers as realistically as possible, *Hollyoaks* developed a hard-hitting storyline about Natasha's unwitting foray into the world of drugs. Natasha's death would prove to be a milestone for the show – not only making front-page news, but also marking a permanent change in the show's direction.

> **DID YOU KNOW...?**
>
> Lucy's party contained over 200 extras, the largest number used at any one time in the show.

The untimely death of Natasha took place at Lucy Benson's eighteenth birthday party. Natasha's date for the evening was the dashing Dermot, who was keen to make sure that she had a night to remember. Dermot's friend Rob Hawthorne, suggested that they drop a tablet into Natasha's drink, so that she would lose all her inhibitions. Rob and Dermot watched as Natasha stormed the dance floor, but were mortified to see her suddenly collapse in a heap. Natasha later died in hospital. It was this event that sparked off the battle between Rob Hawthorne and the residents of Hollyoaks, with several more tragedies to follow...

> **DID YOU KNOW...?**
>
> This episode scored over 2.1 million viewers – the highest rating since the first episode!

Natasha's death had a profound effect on the characters in the show. It marked the beginning of several different stories, as each character tried to find a way of dealing with the tragedy. Phil Redmond described the impact: 'Natasha's death depicts the stark reality of unnecessary death coming very close to one group of friendly and fun-loving people for the first time in their lives and how this is bound to change their outlook in many ways.' Not only did Natasha's death change the course of the show, it also changed the lives of our seven characters as, for the first time ever, they had to face up to the death of someone they'd grown up with.

MAY 1996

Kurt, Bazz and Jambo make plans for the summer, but Tony tells them that he doesn't want to leave Julie. Meanwhile, the mysterious Susi intrigues Ollie and Stan, and is persuaded to go on a camping trip with them. Dermot turns to Rob for help with his finances and they steal computer chips from Mr Benson's car. Meanwhile, Jude organizes a fashion show at the College and Louise falls for Tree, a New Age traveller and leaves Hollyoaks. Michael, an old flame of Maddie's, turns up and gets an unwelcome reception. Meanwhile, Dawn finally plucks up the courage to see her daughter, watching her from a distance while Jambo stands close by to provide a shoulder to cry on.

JUNE 1996

Mr and Mrs Cunningham are at war over custody of Max and Cindy, with Terry trying to cause trouble. Michael and Maddie go out for dinner and reminisce about better times. Ruth and Kurt are finding it difficult living under the same roof and Ollie doesn't understand why Susi hasn't responded to any of his letters. Tony is persuaded to go on holiday with the boys and Jambo books them a trip to Ibiza. Dawn finally confesses to her father about her adopted daughter and has a heart-to-heart with Jambo, but they decide that they're better off as friends. Jude and Ruth decide to give Tony an image overhaul. This provokes a jealous fit from Julie and she calls off the engagement.

JULY 1996

Ruth and Kurt take their motorcycle tests – but Kurt fails. Jude, Dawn and Lewis move into a flat above the video shop, and Lewis organizes a raft race. Lucy has an argument with Rob, who was high on drugs, and they break up again. When Kurt and Jambo find out, they go to the raft race and drag Rob out of his boat so that Stan, Ollie and Susi win. Rob manages to persuade Lucy to go back out with him – she warns him that this is his last chance. Kurt turns down Ruth's invitation for him to join her in the States for the summer and they split up. Despite their split, Kurt is devastated when he realizes Ruth has already gone before he could say goodbye. Meanwhile, Tony decides to head up to Scotland to sort things out with Julie and is gutted when he finds her with another man.

In July 1996 it was announced that *Hollyoaks* had been recommissioned by Channel 4 and would be shown twice-weekly from September. Because of this, *Hollyoaks* was taken off air over the summer so that Mersey Television could make enough episodes to meet the increase in demand. *Hollyoaks* returned in spectacular fashion on 23 September 1996 with a special episode featuring the boys on holiday in Ibiza (see page 76).

The Cunninghams. Front row (left to right): Angela and Gordon; back row (left to right): Jude, Cindy, Max, Dawn.

SEPTEMBER 1996

Tony gets to the airport in just enough time, but is in no mood for a holiday. However, much fun is had in Ibiza, especially by Tony. On their way home from Ibiza, Tony is preoccupied by an annoying itch in his nether regions. Meanwhile, Rob and Lucy return from their holiday and Rob slips something into Lucy's bag, which we later find out to be drugs. Julie and Tony finally sort out their differences, but Tony is evasive when she asks about his holiday. Jude is concerned when she finds a lump in her breast and Ollie, Stan, Cindy and Susi go camping.

ROB AND DERMOT'S CAR CRASH

Written by Claire Phillips
Directed by Bill Gilmour and David Andrews
Broadcast 7 and 11 November 1996

'*Hollyoaks* turns Hollywood tonight with a stunning car crash sequence'
Peter Grant, *The Liverpool Echo*

Featuring one of the most spectacular stunts ever included in the show, Rob and Dermot's car crash was one of the most dramatic episodes of 1996, with their car ending up in the River Dee.

> **DID YOU KNOW...?**
> The windscreen of the car came out and hit the stuntman on the head. He had to go to hospital and have eight stitches!

Following the fallout from Natasha's death, Rob (Warren Derosa) and Dermot (Lauren Beales) continued to embrace a life of crime and, after Dermot confessed to Rob that he was being pursued by angry creditors, Rob hatched the plan to burgle his dealer's lock-up. Rob decided to take Lucy and Carol along to act as unwitting alibis, and the robbery was going to plan until the dealer caught them. They managed to get back into their car, but were then chased through the streets of Chester with Carol and Lucy begging them to stop. Dermot tried to throw the bag of money out of the window and, in trying to stop him, Rob was distracted from driving. He lost control of the car and it plunged into the River Dee. Viewers had to wait a whole nail-biting week to learn the outcome of the crash. Dermot had been killed outright, but Rob, Carol and Lucy managed to survive, although Carol was in a critical condition.

> **DID YOU KNOW...?**
> The episode following the car crash attracted the highest rating for the show since the first episode.

Dermot was victim number two for Rob, with several more to come over the years. The only positive thing to come out of the crash was that Carol's near-death experience sparked off her belief that she might be psychic!

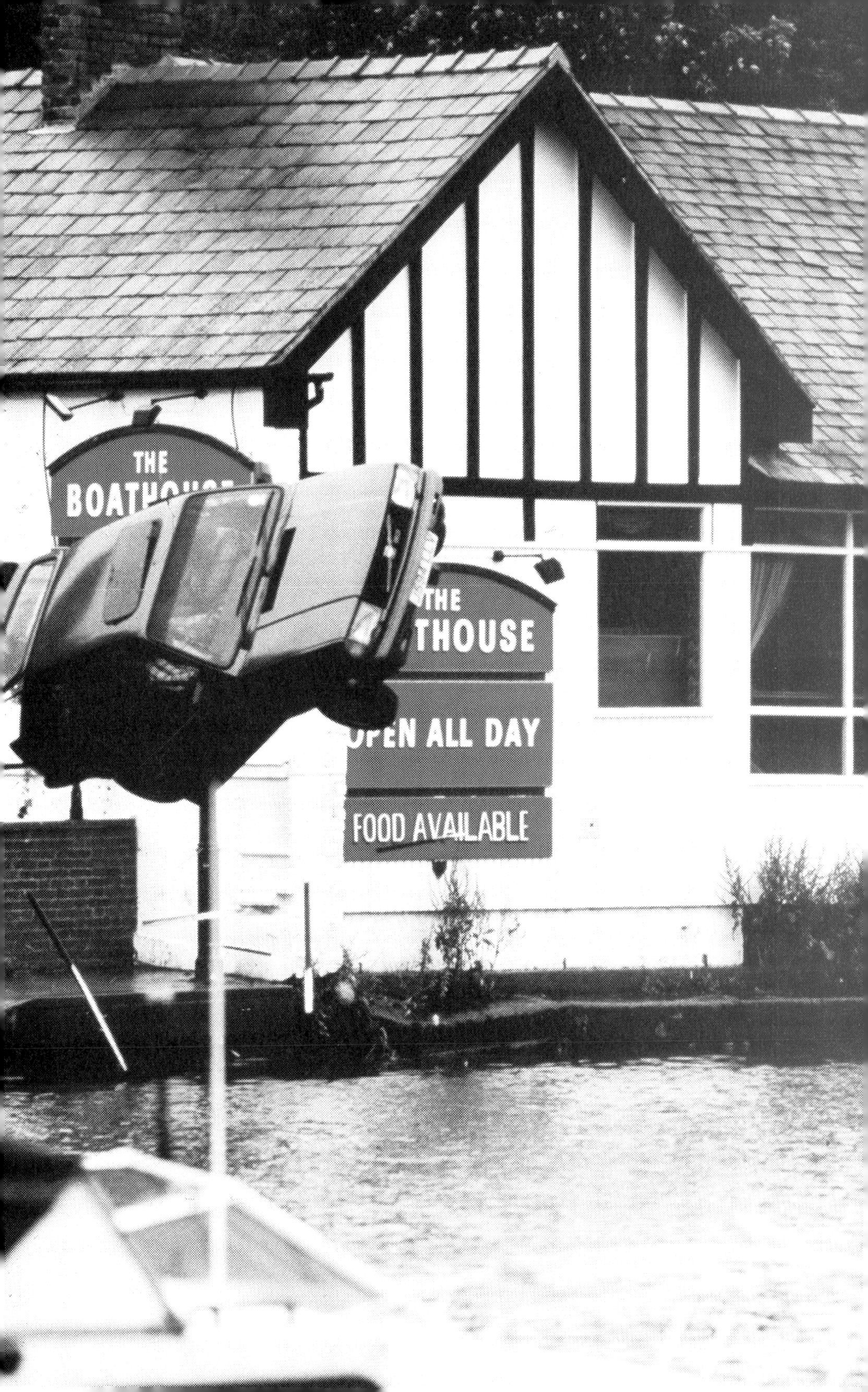
THE
THOUSE
OPEN ALL DAY
FOOD AVAILABLE

OCTOBER 1996

Kurt takes his bike test again, but fails when Tony interrupts him in the middle of it! Cindy finds out Susi can't read and offers to help her learn. Jude is relieved to be given the all-clear and Dawn is a reluctant guest at her mother's wedding to Terry. Ollie has a barbecue to celebrate his GCSE results and gets together with Mandy Richardson. He is later shocked to discover he risks being charged with statutory rape as Mandy is only fifteen. Maddie and Michael's relationship is going well, but she becomes concerned over his jealous behaviour. Jambo inherits a car, which he calls *Beryl*, and Bazz joins Lucy and Carol's band. Dermot has money problems and Rob makes plans to rob a drug dealer's lock-up. Meanwhile, Ruth and Kurt make up and Ruth announces that her family will be taking over The Dog in the Pond.

NOVEMBER 1996

Rob and Dermot raid the lock-up – with fatal consequences. Lucy ends up confessing all to the police but is told that they don't have enough evidence to charge Rob. Newly-wed Mrs Cunningham is rushed into hospital because of a lump in her breast and ends up having the breast removed. Upset by the news of her mother's condition, Dawn turns to Jambo and they end up kissing. However, Dawn insists that they remain just good friends. Meanwhile, at Michael's instruction, Maddie begins to dress more conservatively and Dawn and Jude find out that Terry has 'done a runner', leaving their mother with debts of over £55,000!

DECEMBER 1996

Kurt, Jambo, Lucy and Carol follow Rob on a night's 'work' in the hope that he might incriminate himself. When they finally catch up with him, they personally deliver Rob to the drug dealers from whom he had stolen money. The dealers end up throwing Rob off the roof of a car park, injuring one of his legs. Michael sees Maddie with another man and reacts violently. Ollie continues to see Mandy, despite warnings from Lewis and Ruth becomes editor of the college magazine. Jude becomes interested in Michael and his wallet, but his affections remain with Maddie. Dawn is shocked to learn that her daughter Bethany has kidney failure and that she is her last hope… However, Dawn finds out she isn't compatible, so Mr C offers his kidney instead.

JANUARY 1997

Mr C fails as a match for Dawn's daughter, so she has to contact the child's father, Jack Osborne! He's shocked as he hadn't even known about the pregnancy. He is a match, though, and has the operation. However, Ruth sees Jack with Dawn and he has to confess all. Maddie is concerned about Michael's obsessive behaviour and confronts his parents, but they refuse to believe her until Jude and

Maddie show them a wedding dress Michael has sent Maddie. Tony is devastated when he sees Julie kissing Bruce, her bike instructor, and decides to end their relationship. Ollie and Stan go on a double date with Mandy and Cindy.

FEBRUARY 1997

Ruth tells Dawn that she doesn't want to see her again after finding out about Dawn and Jack. Lucy discovers Bazz is gay and Lewis and Jack react violently, with Lewis using his fists and Jack banning him from The Dog. Julie and Tony continue to fight, especially when Julie discovers the photos of Tony in Ibiza. Jude and Maddie are subjected to a terrifying siege by Michael which ends in Michael's death. Jambo begins dating Anita, Carol's sister, just as Dawn decides to tell him how she feels about him. Carol becomes interested in auras and believes that she might be psychic after her accident.

MARCH 1997

Jude consoles Maddie over Michael's death but Maddie decides to go away to come to terms with it all. Kurt has trouble with a guy called Spike, who works with him on the building site. Spike takes a shine to Ruth and tries to entrap her, but Kurt intervenes and accidentally pushes Spike off the scaffolding. Mandy confesses to Ollie that her father hits her and Lewis. Bazz struggles to come to terms with his sexuality and is viciously attacked outside The Dog, and Kurt and Jambo find out that it was Spike's doing. Tony and Julie are still at loggerheads and Tony starts dating a girl called Marilyn.

Kurt fights with Spike at the top of the scaffolding.

THE SIEGE

Written by Anna Clements
Directed by David Richardson
Broadcast 27 February and 3 March 1997

The siege of Maddie (Yasmin Bannerman) and Jude (Davinia Taylor) by Michael St. John Thomas (Tom Hudson) was an extremely dramatic and suspenseful episode that explored the story of a mentally ill man, desperate to marry the love of his life.

The story of Michael and Maddie's romance had been building for some time, with Michael finally wooing Maddie back after proving to her that he was divorced. Maddie had tentatively entered into a relationship with Michael, yet he soon started to demonstrate fleeting moments of rage and jealousy. Maddie soon grew tired of Michael's abuse and called it all off, later discovering that he was mentally ill. Michael then got together with the man-hungry Jude, who was keen to get her hands on his wallet. However, Michael lost interest in her, returned his affections to Maddie, and became increasingly obsessed with making Maddie his wife.

The siege episode begins with Maddie and Jude being lured into a stable at Michael's house. The girls are then met by Michael, brandishing a shotgun. Kurt and Ruth soon become concerned about Maddie's absence and head towards Michael's house. When Kurt spots Maddie's car hidden under a sheet, he realizes that something is seriously wrong. While they look for more clues, they come across Michael, but Kurt decides not to confront him about Maddie and tells him they are heading home. Kurt alerts the police and when they arrive, gunshots are heard coming from the stable. The police storm the stable to find two dead horses and no sign of Michael, Maddie or Jude.

Michael had taken Maddie and Jude hostage and driven them both to Scotland with the intention of marrying Maddie at Loch Lomond. What follows is a dramatic hostage situation, with Ruth and Kurt waiting

tentatively with the police for Michael to release Maddie and Jude. When Maddie refuses to put on the wedding dress and go through the charade of a marriage to Michael, he takes Jude up to the roof as revenge. For a moment it looks as if Michael is about to push Jude, but when Maddie comes up to the roof dressed in the wedding dress, he is distracted. As Jude manages to escape his clutches, Michael falls to his death.

DID YOU KNOW...?

The siege also has a footnote in *Hollyoaks*'s history for being the first 'bubble' episode – an episode where the show changes location but continues with a story that has already been established.

APRIL 1997

Kurt is charged with assaulting Spike and tries to explain to the police that it was an accident. Tony and Julie take drastic measures and end up splitting the video shop in half. Mandy tells Cindy about her father's drinking. Maddie returns to Hollyoaks and tells Jude that she wants to expand Parkers. Still struggling for cash, Jude begins working for an escort agency and Dawn and Ruth are finally reconciled. Mandy and Cindy start taking the contraceptive pill. Lucy takes pity on a homeless man, then realizes it's Rob! Susi feels sorry for Rob and offers him a room.

MAY 1997

Tony splits up with Marilyn and is soon back with Julie – and once again they decide they want to spend the rest of their lives together. Kurt becomes paranoid that Ruth thinks he's guilty and he breaks up with her and goes away to Hull. Ruth follows him and they end up getting married in true Benson style. Mr Richardson finds out that Mandy and Cindy have been collecting for a donkey sanctuary and the girls are terrified that he will find out that they have been keeping the money. Cindy sleeps with Stan at her sixteenth birthday party and confesses to Mandy that she hasn't been taking the Pill. Meanwhile, Bazz discovers he needs a brain operation following his attack and heads to the Lake District with Lucy to get away from it all. Bazz talks openly about his sexuality, but the day ends in disaster when Bazz falls and hits his head.

JUNE 1997

Bazz is rushed into hospital and has surgery, which successfully cures him. Meanwhile, *Hollyoaks* covers Kurt's trial over a special series of four nights. Jude's debts are mounting and she tries to blackmail Jack, but ends up getting drunk and telling everyone in The Dog about Dawn's child. Jack tries to explain to his wife, but she heads off back to America and takes Darren with her. Susi flies into a jealous rage when she sees Rob with Lucy and tries to stab Lucy, but ends up striking Rob. Mr Richardson finds out about Mandy and Cindy's hoax charity and hits Mandy. Cindy still hasn't had her period and Mandy encourages her to take a pregnancy test. Jambo turns to his dad's wife, Lisa, for advice on Anita, but they end up kissing... And as Bazz goes to say goodbye to Lucy, they end up kissing too, leaving him more confused than ever.

JULY 1997

Maddie has been finding it hard to get over Michael's death and is becoming increasingly insecure about her safety. Jude is still feeling alienated from her family, who can't forgive her for her behaviour, and Cindy is shocked to learn that she is pregnant. Lewis joins Carol, Bazz and Lucy's band and The Crazy Bazz Studs line-up is complete. Jambo's mixed feelings for his stepmother, Lisa, continue and things get more complicated when Jambo finds out his dad is having an affair with his mother. When Lisa finds out, she reveals all about her affair with Jambo.

AUGUST 1997

Tony's wedding day arrives, but at the altar Julie tells him that she can't go through with it. His initial shock turns to relief and he celebrates at The Dog. Cindy despairs when her family don't seem to have time to listen to her problems. Jude's drinking has dramatic consequences when she knocks over a candle and she and Maddie are locked in the flat. Jambo tries to come to terms with his father getting back together with his mother, as well as his feelings for his stepmother. Tony decides to take his honeymoon and goes to Newquay with the gang and ends up sleeping with Carol.

SEPTEMBER 1997

The Crazy Bazz Studs celebrate getting a record contract. Bazz ends up kissing the band's A&R man, Matt, but they are interrupted by Lewis, who warns Bazz to tell Lucy – or he will. Cindy pretends to Mandy that she's had an abortion. Meanwhile, Jambo moves out of his mum's and shares a flat with Tony, but they argue like an old married couple. Lewis talks to his mother, Helen, about his concerns over his father's drinking and violence. Meanwhile, Mr Richardson discovers Mandy has modelled for the college magazine and warns her not to pursue it. Mandy's problems continue when she sees Ollie with another girl and they split up, causing Mandy to become increasingly obsessed with her weight.

OCTOBER 1997

Still overwhelmed with fears about her pregnancy, Cindy takes her anger out on Stan and tells him everything. Stan takes the news badly and ends up in a crash, with Ollie as his passenger. Cindy tries to throw herself down the stairs in a desperate attempt to miscarry. Meanwhile, Ruth's problems continue when she finds out Spike is one of the builders doing repairs to the college. Spike traps Ruth in a room and tries to force himself on her, but she is rescued when Rob intervenes. Jambo catches Dawn giving Jack an innocent kiss and jumps to the conclusion that they are having an affair. They soon make up and Dawn admits to Jambo she's been feeling unwell and has been to the doctor's.

NOVEMBER 1997

Jill Patrick arrives as a new barmaid at The Dog and there is an instant spark between her and Jack Osborne. However, Jack gets more than he bargained for when Jill's children – Sol, Gina and Kate – appear on the scene. He feels compelled to offer them a room when he hears about their problems. Meanwhile, Jambo unveils his new bed to Dawn, but their happiness is short-lived when Dawn discovers she has leukaemia. Mandy has problems with her father when

STAN AND OLLIE'S DEATH

Written by Anna Clements
Directed by David Crean
Broadcast 6 October 1997

As Kurt's annoying little brother, Ollie (Paul Leyshon) has provided *Hollyoaks* with some of its great comedy moments, ranging from hiding the 'Unidentified Bleeping Object' in Kurt's room, where it proceeded to wake Kurt up at 6.59am every morning, to his career as a roving journalist for the Riverbank Review, instigating such seminal reports as 'Babe of the Month' and 'Cleavage of the Year.'

Every comedian needs a sidekick and to complete the double act, Ollie had canteen worker Stan (Nathan Valente). Even after Ollie exposed the 'Chips for Sex' scandal, insinuating that Stan gave girls extra chips in order to seduce them, Ollie and Stan remained the best of friends and were always a force to be reckoned with. Whilst Ollie saw his fair share of dramas – in

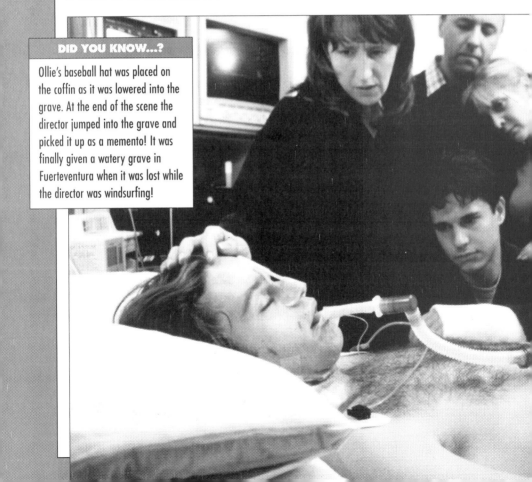

DID YOU KNOW...?

Ollie's baseball hat was placed on the coffin as it was lowered into the grave. At the end of the scene the director jumped into the grave and picked it up as a memento! It was finally given a watery grave in Fuerteventura when it was lost while the director was windsurfing!

particular, the prospect of facing a charge for statutory rape as a result of sleeping with Mandy, not discovering until later that she was only fifteen – he had a remarkably vibrant

> 'Stan and I were the original comedy duo…we just did all the silly things that you always wished you could do as a kid.'

spirit and refused to let anything get him down. The same could be said for Stan, although his world was turned upside down when he discovered that he had got Cindy Cunningham pregnant on her sixteenth birthday.

Stan was desperate to prove to Cindy that he would stand by her during her pregnancy, but an emotional Cindy told Stan that she hated him and wanted nothing to do with him. Stan was devastated and sped off in his car to The Dog, where he began drinking heavily. Ollie soon came to his rescue, but Stan seemed beyond help and headed back to his car with Ollie in tow. Lucy urged Kurt, Tony and Bazz to follow Stan's car, worried for Ollie's safety. Despite Ollie's warnings, Stan refused to slow down, taking his frustration out on the car. Stan had no time to brake as they suddenly came across a lorry reversing down the road. The car hurtled into the lorry and Stan and Ollie suffered multiple injuries. Kurt, Tony and Bazz were also injured in the car

behind, but all eyes were on Stan and Ollie – surely the two most popular characters weren't going to die?

The audience's fears were confirmed when, the following week, both Stan and Ollie died in hospital. The Benson family had often been perceived as the perfect nuclear family – three beautiful children with two loving parents, but this all changed on the day that Ollie died. After his death, Lucy spiralled out of control, turning to drugs to overcome her grief and guilt over the part she had played in Ollie's death. The accident put incredible pressure on Mr and Mrs Benson's marriage and, although they managed to get over their problems, tragedy was to strike them once more with their eldest son Kurt dying in a jet ski accident.

> 'It was a great way to go. I came in with a bang and went out with a bang – I couldn't have wished for a better way to go.'

he slaps her in school and Mandy and her mother take refuge in Lewis's flat. Lucy is upset to find out that Bazz has been having an affair with Matt and ends up turning to Rob. Mr C's shady cousin, Benny, arrives and immediately hooks up with Jude. Cindy is finding it increasingly difficult to hide her pregnancy from her parents and is forced to wear baggy clothes.

DECEMBER 1997

Dawn undergoes chemotherapy for her leukaemia and is anxious for Jambo to go on tour with the band, although she's ill. Kurt and Ruth continue to argue, especially about spending Christmas with Ruth's family. It goes from bad to worse when they realize they will be spending it with the Patricks. However, Kate is pleased, having taken a shine to Kurt. Tony is dating three women – all of whom invite him round for Christmas Day! Dawn tragically dies on Christmas Day. At the same time, Cindy ends up giving birth in the video shop and abandons her baby. When the Cunninghams find out, they begin to pick up the pieces. Lucy finds herself feeling isolated from her family. She turns once again to Rob for support, who offers her tranquillizers.

JANUARY 1998

Cindy announces that she wants to have her baby, Holly, adopted. Jambo is finding it difficult to come to terms with Dawn's death. He becomes isolated from his friends and quits the band. Jack is struggling with having the Patricks at The Dog, especially when he learns about an intimidation campaign against Gina. Ruth is forced to give Rob a job on the college newspaper, despite Kurt's efforts. Mr and Mrs Benson become further estranged as they both struggle to come to terms with Ollie's death. Lucy is finding it difficult to cope and continues to take tranquillizers from Rob. Meanwhile, Lewis discovers that Mandy has been taking slimming pills and Jude continues to steal cars for Benny.

FEBRUARY 1998

Lucy has become addicted to tranquillizers. Gina is arrested when she fails to testify in a hearing about a stabbing she witnessed and Jill decides it would be better if the family moved away. Jack is against this and asks Jill to marry him – much to the shock of Ruth and Sol! Rob has organized a hill walk in Wales and when Ruth has another argument with Kurt, she ends up going with Lewis. Carol is paired off with Kevin, Lucy with Rob and Lewis goes off with Ruth. Anxious to win, Kevin moves the trail flags and takes a short cut. Disaster strikes when Kevin breaks his leg and Rob and Lucy get lost. Ruth and Lewis take refuge in a cave and end up kissing… Meanwhile, Jude becomes proprietor of Parkers and Max and O.B. take Holly out in an attempt to find a girlfriend.

MARCH 1998

Lucy begins to realize she might be addicted to tranquillizers, but can't cope without them. Meanwhile, the Benson's marriage hits the rocks when Mrs Benson announces that she wants another child. Jill Patrick and Jack Osborne get married. The family meet Kate's boyfriend, Richard, and are shocked that he is twice her age! Helen and Mandy call round to see Mr Richardson and are shocked when they see where he is living. Mandy tells him she's in trouble at school and he offers to tutor her. Tony has problems when his ex-girlfriend, Tessie, turns up and tells him that she's pregnant and wants money! Benny finds out that Jude now owns Parkers and reminds her that she still owes him money – she either pays him or he comes in as partner. Meanwhile, Carol buys Jambo's car *Beryl*…

APRIL 1998

Jambo takes Tony's advice and becomes a landscape gardener. Tony gives Tessie some money and then finds out that she was lying and this had been her revenge against him for dumping her. A desperate Cindy tries to suffocate baby Holly, but is interrupted by Jude, who takes Holly to hospital. Cindy begins to

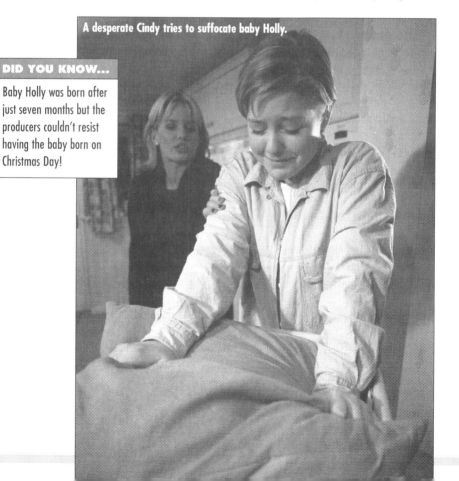

A desperate Cindy tries to suffocate baby Holly.

DID YOU KNOW…

Baby Holly was born after just seven months but the producers couldn't resist having the baby born on Christmas Day!

DAWN'S DEATH

Written by Neil Jones and Lucy Gough
Directed by Jo Hallows
Broadcast 22 and 29 December 1997

If there is one story that is guaranteed to infuriate an audience, it is when two characters who seem destined to be together are unable to acknowledge their feelings. This was most certainly the theme of the burgeoning relationship between Dawn Cunningham (Lisa Williamson) and James 'Jambo' Bolton (Will Mellor). Since the show began, these two remained the closest of friends and, although they had their fair share of near misses, they never quite managed to get together. It was only in 1997 that this changed, when they finally realized that they were meant to spend the rest of their lives together. However, their happiness was tragically cut short when Dawn discovered that she had leukaemia. What followed was one of the most moving love stories ever depicted by *Hollyoaks*.

On Christmas Day, at Dawn's request, they hired a rowing boat. As Jambo proposed to her, Dawn finally lost her battle against leukaemia and died in his arms. We were left with the heartrending image of a helpless Jambo in the middle of the river, holding Dawn in his arms. The following week's episode focussed on the effect of Dawn's death on the Cunningham family and we were once again reminded of Jambo's pain when he broke down whilst performing the eulogy at Dawn's funeral.

With touching performances from both Lisa Williamson and Will Mellor, the story of Dawn and Jambo remains one of the most popular and moving love stories in *Hollyoaks*'s history.

> **DID YOU KNOW...?**
>
> The writer, Lucy Gough, has been dubbed the 'funeral queen' because she's written more funeral episodes than any other *Hollyoaks* writer! Her most recent was Lewis's funeral in October 2001.

> **DID YOU KNOW...?**
>
> Series producer Jo Hallows directed these episodes and admits that she almost lost Lisa Williamson (Dawn) and Will Mellor (Jambo) when their rowing boat headed precariously close to the weir!

> **DID YOU KNOW...?**
>
> Writer Neil Jones has his own special memory of this episode: 'This was only my second episode and I was eager to find out what people thought of it – so I was chuffed when, the morning after it was broadcast, I overheard some lads at the bus stop saying how brilliant it was... I was pretty pleased with myself until I discovered that they were mainly impressed by a scene in which you could allegedly see Dawn's pants...'

MANDY'S STORY

Almost two years before *Hollyoaks* broke new boundaries with its depiction of male rape, the show received praise for its sensitive treatment of another taboo – child abuse. This was the horrific story of Mandy Richardson, powerfully played by a teenage Sarah Dunn, who suffered both physical and sexual abuse at the hands of her alcoholic father, Dennis (David McAlister).

Mandy had run away to London after another incident with her father and had reached such a low ebb that she was contemplating suicide. At that time, her family were unaware of Mandy's problems, and Mr Richardson repeated his chilling denial of having done anything untoward. When Lewis (Ben Hull) finally heard the news that Mandy was in hospital, he rushed to her bedside and, after much probing, she finally broke down and told him what her father had been doing to her for the majority of her life. A devastated Lewis promised Mandy that he would never let him hurt her again.

What followed was a heartbreaking portrayal of Mandy's struggle to find the courage to go to the police and report her father. She finally managed to do this and, despite Mr Richardson's various attempts at forcing her to drop the charges, the case finally reached the courts. He was found guilty and sentenced to seven years' imprisonment.

Mandy's journey to come to terms with what her father did to her, as well as what Lewis did to himself, is one that continues to this day. Thankfully, Mandy's nightmare had a happy ending when she finally saw her father locked away and she could begin her life again. Sadly, this wasn't to be the case for Lewis.

DID YOU KNOW...?

David McAlister, the actor who played Dennis Richardson, was so convincing in his role that he received hate mail!

realize that she couldn't bear to lose Holly and decides to keep her. Richard tells Kate he wants to leave his wife and they make plans for the future. Mr Richardson starts helping Mandy with her revision and Mandy is certain he's changed and asks her mother to let him stay with them. Lewis is suspicious of Benny and confronts him, prompting Benny to tell him all about Jude's criminal activities. Lewis is upset that Jude lied to him and breaks up with her.

MAY 1998

Richard tells Kate that he wants them to move away together, but Kate's delight soon fades when he fails to turn up and so she turns to Kurt for support… Meanwhile, Mandy is happy having Mr Richardson back at the house but things soon turn nasty when Mr Richardson sees Mandy with boyfriend, Sol. Mr Richardson reprimands Mandy and grabs her. We see the door closing behind them and Mandy dreading what is to come. Elsewhere, Jude confronts Benny and threatens to go to the police – he ends up clearing everything out of Parkers, leaving Jude facing financial ruin. Lucy's addiction continues and she messes up a quotation for a big computer order from Mr Benson's company. Tony sees a girl, Jasmine, at a barn dance and is immediately smitten.

JUNE 1998

The Richardsons start panicking when Mandy disappears. Mr Richardson implicates Sol and the police are suspicious that he doesn't have an alibi for the night Mandy went missing. Meanwhile, Jambo makes preparations to leave Hollyoaks as he has a gardening job in Anglesey. Tony is completely besotted with Jasmine, but gets paranoid, suspecting that she might be a prostitute. He later finds out she's a personal trainer! Ruth and Kurt move in together and Tony finds a vagrant in Jambo's shed, in the shape of Finn, an old friend of Jambo's! Kurt and Rob both compete for the lifeguard's job, but Rob loses out when he begins to struggle in the water because of his leg injury and Kurt has to rescue him. Later, Rob finds out that his father has died and takes the news badly – he turns to heroin to get him through…

JULY 1998

The Richardsons discover that withdrawals have been taken from Mandy's bank account in London and hope she might be there. Despite this, Sol is arrested by the police and, at Jack's instigation, Sol admits that he had been joyriding the night Mandy went missing. Meanwhile, Mr Benson suffers a heart attack, but luckily manages to pull through. Lucy feels ostracized by her family and turns to Rob – she needs relief and he offers her heroin… Tony is shocked to discover that Jasmine also has an eye for the ladies. Meanwhile, Ruth goes to London on a work placement, leaving Kurt home alone. Following an impromptu party at his flat, Kurt ends up kissing Kate and is immediately racked with guilt. Sol gets a call from Mandy but no one believes it was genuine. Gina and Cindy defy their parents and go to a music festival. Mr C goes after them, but ends up sampling some space cakes and stays for the festival!

AUGUST 1998

The gang head off to Anglesey to see Jambo, and Kurt and Kate use the trip to spend some time alone. However, their plans are ruined when Ruth turns up for a surprise visit. Disaster strikes when *Beryl* goes rolling off a cliff! Meanwhile, the search for Mandy continues, with both Lewis and Mr Richardson looking for her in London. Just as they are about to give up, they discover that Mandy is working in a Soho strip club. Mr Richardson goes in and comes face to face with Mandy, who quickly runs away. The police inform the Richardsons that Mandy was spotted on a bridge and that her coat was later found in the river. They immediately panic that Mandy may have killed herself. Their fears are compounded when Helen gets a letter of apology from Mandy. Lucy is becoming increasingly desperate for heroin and, despite Rob's warnings, she goes behind his back to try and get some.

SEPTEMBER 1998

Kurt and Kate are almost caught in the act when Ruth arrives back unannounced from London. Lucy is still in a desperate state and her addiction compels her to steal from the Bensons' business. However, Rob refuses to tolerate her addiction and gives Lucy an ultimatum – it's either him or the heroin. Rob has further problems with his bad leg and is told that he might one day lose it. Meanwhile, Sol is devastated by the news of Mandy's 'suicide' and insists that Mr Richardson is to blame. However, in Mandy's absence, Sol ends up getting together with Cindy. Mr Richardson plans a memorial service for Mandy, but Helen refuses to accept that she's gone. Jude plans a booze run to France, but her plans are ruined when she discovers Max and O.B. have stowed away in the back of the van!

OCTOBER 1998

Lewis finds out that Mandy is alive and in hospital, and rushes to her bedside. A devastated Mandy confesses to Lewis that her father raped her. Meanwhile, Kate and Kurt continue their affair, despite the added danger that both Tony and Jasmine know about them. Jude is alerted to the fact that she needs to raise £10,000 by the end of the month if she wants to keep Parkers and ends up arranging to transport a stolen car to France. Meanwhile, to pay for drugs, Rob has managed to procure £10,000 from Lucy, who has raided Ollie's insurance money and the Bensons' business. Rob takes revenge on Kurt by injecting heroin into an already drugged-up Lucy. He then takes her to the roof of the car park where he was thrown off and announces that 'It's pay-back time,' leaving

'OFF ON ONE', THE VIDEO EXCLUSIVE

Released October 1998
Written by Phil Redmond
Directed by Jo Hallows

Did you ever wonder what happened on the mysterious weekend that Rob and Kurt disappeared to France? For all those who never bought the video, what follows is the final piece of the jigsaw – the details of what went on between Rob and Kurt that made Rob intent on seeking vengeance, an obsession that was eventually to put several lives in jeopardy...

In October 1998, *Hollyoaks* produced its first spin-off movie. *Hollyoaks: Off on One* was made exclusively for video release. It was undoubtedly *Hollyoaks* with a dose of Hollywood, including countless car chases, boat chases and some superb stunts shot on location in the beautiful Honfleur in Normandy. All the ingredients for the perfect Hollywood movie were included – action, adventure, comedy and romance – with Ruth and Lewis throwing caution to the wind and expressing their feelings for each other.

The back-story for the video was Rob Hawthorne's vendetta against Kurt Benson for the leg injury he had received when his drug dealers threw him off the roof of a car park. Rob had always blamed Kurt for leaving him at their mercy and his slow-burning plan for revenge came to a head when he managed to get Lucy hooked on heroin. On the eve of the weekend that is covered by the video, Rob had caused Lucy to overdose on heroin and she had been taken to intensive care. Kurt followed Rob to France, intent on revenge...

Going to France were Carol and Jude, who were on a booze run for Parkers, and Tony, Lewis and Ruth, who were desperate to prevent Kurt from doing something he might later regret. In France a spectacular chase between Rob and Kurt took place, climaxing in Rob stealing a speedboat, and Kurt managing to climb on board just before he sped off. A fight ensued – Rob charged at Kurt, who quickly stepped to one side, causing Rob to plunge into the water. Refusing to listen to Rob's pleas, Kurt drove off, leaving him floating in the middle of the Atlantic. As Kurt drove off in the boat, he delivered the unforgettable line to Rob: 'You believe in fate, don't you? Well, if you make it, that's fate and if you don't? That's fate too…'

Off On One certainly had the X-factor and by the end of 1998 had sold over 135,000 copies. It marked the beginning of Rob's relentless pursuit of revenge on Kurt and his friends, which would reach its peak in a spectacular episode on the eve of the new Millennium.

Lucy in a coma. Luckily, Kurt finds her in just enough time and Lucy is taken to hospital. As Lucy's condition begins to improve, the Bensons discover that she has stolen £10,000 from them.

The video exclusive, *Off On One*, takes place over the weekend that Jude goes to France and Kurt heads off in pursuit of Rob for revenge.

NOVEMBER 1998
Jude discovers £10,000 in the van that she took to France and realizes Rob must have left it there. Carol realizes it must be the money that Rob stole from Lucy and offers it back to the Bensons. Mandy finally goes to the police to report her father and he is arrested, but granted bail. Mr Richardson tries to force Mandy to drop the charges, but she refuses. Facing ruin, Jude is forced to contact Benny, who offers to help her with the money if she gets married to a friend of his. Kurt is torn between Ruth and Kate, but the affair gets dangerous when Jill begins to suspect something. Jude finds out that Benny's marriage plan is a ruse to steal an expensive necklace and the heist goes wrong, leaving Jude as the main suspect. Mr Richardson is found guilty of rape and is sentenced to seven years in jail.

DECEMBER 1998
Jude has no choice but to leave the country – with Dawn's passport. Ruth is devastated when she learns of Kurt's affair and tells him that it's over. Meanwhile, Jack defends Ruth's honour by throwing Kate out of The Dog. Kurt finally persuades Ruth to give him another chance but Kate refuses to accept that it's over between them. Romance blossoms over Christmas for Helen Richardson and Mr C! Finn and Carol finally get together when he presents her with the restored *Beryl* and Lucy announces to Kurt that she wants to know what happened with Rob in France.

JANUARY 1999
Ruth gets into a fight with Kate that ends in Kate trying to drown her. In a fit of rage, Ruth tells Kate that she doesn't have the same father as Sol and Gina. Kurt intervenes, tries to teach Kate a lesson and almost drowns her. In the wake of the fight, Ruth and Kurt do some soul-searching and realize that they're not right for each other, prompting Kurt to leave Hollyoaks. Cindy starts dating a decorator called Sean, but doesn't tell him she has a daughter. Mandy begins driving lessons with Mr C, but it is clear that driving is not Mandy's strong point!

FEBRUARY 1999
Cindy goes on a date with Sean, leaving Holly at home on her own. Mr C arrives home to find Holly just as she's about to fall down the stairs. Lewis rekindles his affair with Ruth, but they agree to keep their relationship under wraps. Lucy

takes more heroin and Carol persuades her to go into rehab, where she meets Clare, a reformed heroin addict. Kate is determined to track down her father, despite warnings not to from her mother. A new lifeguard arrives at the pool in the shape of Adam Morgan and he soon becomes friends with Jasmine. The band is playing a gig when the police arrive, prompting Lucy to hide her drugs in Lewis's guitar case, causing Lewis to get arrested. Finn buys a double-decker bus and moves it into the Yard.

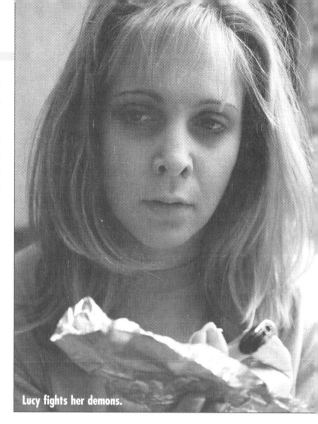
Lucy fights her demons.

MARCH 1999

A furious Lewis confronts Lucy and quits the band. Kate is confused when she is introduced to Joe – the twin brother she never knew she had. Jill finally tells Sol and Gina the truth – she isn't their mother. She took care of them after their real mother committed suicide. Sol and Gina are furious that their 'mother' has lied to them. Mandy offers to model for Mr C's driving school and Jasmine is bored with Tony and ends up kissing Adam. Jasmine then tells Tony he's boring and they break up. Lucy's friend, Clare, has trouble when her ex-boyfriend and dealer, Ty turns up. Carol opens a clairvoyant stall on Finn's market and Sean moves in to the Cunninghams' and causes friction between Cindy and her mother. Lewis is still pining for Ruth, but they agree to cool things until she's sorted her head out. Meanwhile, Ruth meets Luke Morgan and he seduces her.

APRIL 1999

The Morgan family arrive in Hollyoaks and plan to turn Store 24 into a café. Sol and Jill are arguing in Jill's car when Sol smashes into Store 24 and Jill is seriously injured. Sol suddenly realizes how important she is to him – even if she isn't his mother. Ruth is embarrassed when she discovers Luke is only sixteen and her bad luck continues when she confesses all to Lewis and he dumps her. Clare's troubles with Ty continue. He ends up supplying her with heroin and she accidentally overdoses on it. Her death is a wake-up call for Lucy, who realizes she must get clean. Sol confesses to the police that he was driving Jill's car when it crashed and Gina lashes out at Jill for getting him into trouble.

MAY 1999

Beth Morgan arrives in Hollyoaks and Lewis, Tony and Finn all set their sights on her. Mr and Mrs Benson decide to leave Hollyoaks, but Lucy decides to stay. Meanwhile, Sean makes a play for Mandy and gets heavy with her, leaving Mandy with a dilemma: should she tell Cindy? Tony attends the Hank Ackerman business course, and Sol is up in front of the magistrates, but is frustrated when the case is adjourned. Ruth ends up kissing Jasmine, but immediately regrets it and throws her out of the flat. Mr C advertises his driving school featuring Mandy on the side of Finn's bus. Luke sees the poster and it's love at first sight.

JUNE 1999

Jasmine finally makes up with Ruth, but they agree to remain just friends. Mandy finally goes on a date with Luke and they are immediately besotted with one another. Sol is shocked when he is given a custodial sentence and is sent to prison for four weeks. Tony returns from his conference a changed man and Lewis gets together with Beth. Kate misses Joe and is upset that his father, Dave, won't let him see her. Eventually, to Kate's delight, Joe moves into The Dog. Meanwhile, Lucy believes she has finally beaten her addiction to heroin and Tony is shocked when it is announced that Massive Movies will be opening next door, especially when he finds out it's run by his business guru, Hank Ackerman! Finally, Finn and Lewis dig up a skull in the Yard – whose is it?

JULY 1999

Finn and Lewis discover the skull is Roman and the Yard is closed for excavation. Tony is unable to compete against Massive Movies and is forced to close down. Lewis realizes that Beth is too young for him and he splits up with her. Finn decides to use his double-decker as a tour bus with Carol as the guide. Sol is horrified when his cellmate hangs himself and is glad to be released. There is confusion for Lewis when he finds a pregnancy test kit and assumes it's Mandy's. However, they are both shocked to discover that it's their mother's! Mr C decides to do the honourable thing and proposes to Helen. Ruth decides she wants Lewis back, but he doesn't want to know. Adam gets a surprise when his Australian girlfriend, Kerri, pays him a surprise visit.

AUGUST 1999

The Cunningham and Richardson families are divided over the forthcoming marriage, with Mandy actively against it. Ruth decides there's nothing left for her in Chester and plans to return to the States, offering her flat to Kate. Lewis makes a mad dash to the airport to stop her and Ruth finally agrees to stay, but then realizes that she will have to share with Kate! Cindy is concerned when she finds a bruise on Holly and suspects Max, despite her mother's misgivings about Sean. Adam and Kerri are busy getting reacquainted, but Adam's nose is put out of joint when she hooks up with Finn. The Morgans decide their marriage isn't working and Mr C opens up Drive 'N' Buy.

SEPTEMBER 1999

The gang go with Finn to Ireland and, on their return, Lucy finds out that Kurt has been killed in a jet ski accident. Sean continues to mistreat Holly and Angela throws him out. He leaves for Wales to work on a caravan site and Cindy goes with him. Mr Morgan ends up in a clinch with Kerri and is caught by Rob. To mark the occasion of *Hollyoaks* going out three times a week, Lucy is kidnapped by Rob and taken to a disused watertank, with Ruth, Lewis and Tony in pursuit. We meet the new students of Hollyoaks Community College when Geri, Sam, Nikki, Alex and Anna arrive. Jack Osborne returns home with his son Darren and Beth meets Rob and is immediately smitten.

OCTOBER 1999

The Cunninghams visit Cindy at the caravan park and Mr C tries to pay Sean to leave Cindy. Cindy is furious and throws them out. Tony gets together with Lucy and begins working for Mr Morgan in Deva. Finn and Carol go on a date after Finn loses a bet with Tony and they end up back on the bus, which continues to rock for forty-eight hours! Kate and Joe are confused when they begin to realize they have feelings for each other. Meanwhile, there is a health scare in Halls when Nikki contracts meningitis. Ruth continues to grieve for Kurt, leaving Lewis confused as to what to do. Mr Morgan finally listens to the warnings about Rob and bans Beth from seeing him. Tensions continue between the Osbornes and the Patricks with Sol and Kate at loggerheads with Darren and Ruth. Carol gets the fright of her life when Rob tries to drown her in the bath and tells her that he wants the £10,000 he left in Jude's van.

NOVEMBER 1999

Ruth is becoming suspicious of Kate and Joe's closeness, and shares her feelings with Jill, who doesn't believe her. Kate and Joe decide to run away together, but at the last moment Kate leaves alone. Meanwhile, in the caravan, Holly burns her hand on a firework and Cindy takes her to hospital. Mr C and Max intervene and take Cindy back to Chester. Luke starts football training and has trouble on the pitch with Mark Gibbs when he inadvertently injures Mark's leg. Nikki's boyfriend, Dan, turns up on special leave, causing tension between secret lovers, Sam and Nikki. Jill walks out on Jack when he fails to back her up over family problems. Meanwhile, Adam becomes friendly with his tutor, Christine; Cindy returns to Sean and Carol discovers that she has an STD.

ROB KIDNAPS LUCY, TONY, LEWIS & RUTH

Written by Allan Swift and Neil Jones
Directed by David Richardson
Broadcast 13–16 September 1999

If *Hollyoaks: Off on One* was *Hollyoaks* with a dose of Hollywood, this four-night special, climaxing in Rob kidnapping Lucy, Lewis, Tony and Ruth was undoubtedly 'Hollyoaks: The Disaster Movie'!

In what was one of the most implausible, yet memorable episodes in the history of *Hollyoaks*, Rob returned from the middle of the Atlantic Ocean to kidnap Lucy and take her to a nautical test centre, where he planned to drown her. However, Lewis, Tony and Ruth were on Lucy's trail and, as they reached the tower to rescue her, Rob trapped them

DID YOU KNOW...?

Hollyoaks went four nights for the watertank special, securing the highest ratings for 1999, with a record 2.6 million tuning in on the following Monday to discover the fate of Lucy, Ruth, Lewis and Tony!

in the tank where they found themselves plunged into water with no obvious exit. Rob

stood in the control box playing God – pressing buttons indiscriminately to alter the water temperature and add wave effects. Lucy was beginning to get hypothermia in the tank, provoking Tony to reveal his true feelings for her. Indeed it looked as if they had all met their match. Rob doubted their resilience, but thanks to the bravery of Tony, they managed to escape.

Tony used his valuable air canister to swim to the bottom of the tank, where he found a hatch and managed to get it open. Then, as Robbie Williams's song 'Angels' began to play, Lucy, Ruth, Tony and Lewis were sucked through the hole and found themselves washed up in the River Dee. As they swam to the side, Tony noticed that Lucy hadn't made it back and swam after her, dragging her to the river bank. He performed the kiss of life on her and miraculously, she survived.

Whilst built on an entirely far-fetched premise, the watertank episodes proved a gritty story, with millions of viewers left wondering if the four would get out of the tank alive. All the hard work put in by the cast and crew – who spent the majority of the shoot treading water and trying to keep afloat – paid off when these special episodes earned the highest rating achieved by *Hollyoaks* for the whole of 1999.

DECEMBER 1999

Luke tries to visit Mark in hospital, but is beaten up by Mark's brothers. Sam is taken aback when Nikki reveals that she can't break up with Dan because he's in prison for killing someone in a car accident and it's all her fault. Alex and Sam go to Ireland to trace Alex's Internet girlfriend and Alex is shocked to discover that she has died and her parents have been sending the e-mails. Lucy confronts Rob about Beth and they argue about what he's done to her family. Beth overhears them and breaks up with Rob. Sean tells Cindy that he wants to work in Tenerife and she agrees to go with him. However, she's devastated when she realizes that Holly needs a passport and Sean goes off without her. Jack persuades Jill to come back to The Dog and Jill is shocked to discover Gina is a lesbian. Carol finds a poodle she names 'Meryl' and Finn organizes a Millennium party on his bus. Rob tries to set fire to the bus, but ends up dying in the blast.

JANUARY 2000

The new Millennium opens with Hollyoaks in shock over Rob's death. Lucy is number one suspect, but is cleared when the police find incriminating evidence against Rob. Nikki had also been injured in the blast and boyfriend Dan, newly released from prison comes to visit her, incurring the wrath of Sam, who promptly tells Dan all about their relationship. Meanwhile, Luke continues to have problems with Mark and his brothers and Adam ends up getting together with Geri, but tells her that he doesn't want a relationship. Gina struggles with people's prejudices about her sexuality, especially with Darren, whose friend is standing against her in the student elections. Carol thinks she's won the lottery and insists that Tony dig up his Millennium capsule so she can get her ticket back. Free from Rob, Lucy decides to leave Hollyoaks and go travelling, leaving a heartbroken Tony behind. Lewis starts gambling again and Finn decides to buy himself a barge, but discovers it has a leak while he's in bed with Carol!

FEBRUARY 2000

Luke becomes friends with Darren and they put Mark Gibbs in his place. Finn is desperate to save his sinking barge and organizes for it to be dragged onto dry land. Carol discovers that her beloved dog, Meryl, is an impostor and that Finn had accidentally killed the original. Adam's lecturer, Christine, feels jealous of Geri and rekindles her affair with Adam, only to be interrupted by Ruth and the new newspaper editor, Ed. Christine makes out that Adam was trying to force himself on her. Things look bleak for Adam until Geri and newly appointed assistant caretaker, Matt, testify at the tribunal that it was a consensual affair. Sol finds himself jobless and homeless when he falls out with Jack, and Finn secures a bank loan and goes into partnership with Lewis to buy the Yard from Mr Morgan. Max and Mandy compete for driving lessons and Max passes first time. Tony decides to buy a property, but is taken aback when he finds it has a squatter, in the shape of Sol!

MARCH 2000

Anna is shocked to discover her father has been having an affair and it's front-page news because he's a vicar. The bullying campaign against Luke continues and Darren tries to sort it out by becoming friends with Mark. Alex sets up a webcam in Geri's room and broadcasts it to the whole of the college. In revenge, Geri tells him he can't come on the trip to Switzerland that she's organized. They call a truce on condition that Alex plays maid to them all. Ruth is struggling with her dissertation, so Lewis uses the money Finn had lent him to hire the club to buy her a computer. Dan decides he wants to visit the family of the victim of his driving accident, but doesn't get the reception he'd hoped for. Tony does some building work on his house and finds a painting by Lowry hidden in a wall cavity. Believing it to be a fake, he cuts it up, only to find out it had been worth £14,000! After a match, Luke is the victim of a shocking sex attack and Max finally loses his virginity to Chloe. Finn is attracted to a sophisticated older woman unaware that she is Tony's mother, Victoria! Anna ends up kissing Sam as he comforts her over her father's affair and a new relationship begins.

APRIL 2000

Luke struggles to come to terms with the attack and becomes withdrawn. Finn and Lewis become friendly with local club owner, Lorraine, and Lewis starts gambling in her casino. Sol is reduced to begging and refuses to return to The Dog. The gang go on the skiing trip to Switzerland and Darren takes advantage of Mandy and Luke's disintegrating relationship. Zara's problems at school continue when she sets fire to the art block and is suspended, pending

The gang go skiing in Switzerland.

BREAKING BOUNDARIES – LUKE'S RAPE

Written by Neil Jones
Directed by Jo Hallows
Broadcast 15 March 2000

'Proving that it's not just a show for teenagers… the audacious plotline sensitively addresses male rape – which accounts for a quarter of all sexual abuse cases – an issue rarely discussed, let alone depicted on a popular television show. For that, *Hollyoaks* should be commended.'

Sarah Cohen, *Heat*

Hollyoaks: Breaking Boundaries was undoubtedly the show's greatest moment. It is the most critically acclaimed episode of the soap to date and brought an entirely new audience to the show.

Critics were sharpening their knives when they heard that Hollyoaks was to depict the taboo subject of male rape and attacked the episode even before it had been broadcast. But they were proved wrong by the sensitive and heart-rending depiction of a young boy being sexually abused in the most horrific way.

Billed as 'tantalizing and terrifying', this special episode followed the developing story of Luke Morgan (Gary Lucy), who had been the victim of a

> **DID YOU KNOW...?**
>
> Over 3 million tuned in at 10.55pm to watch this episode, scoring a record 21 per cent share of the evening's audience. This single episode is undoubtedly the most acclaimed of the *Hollyoaks* back catalogue.

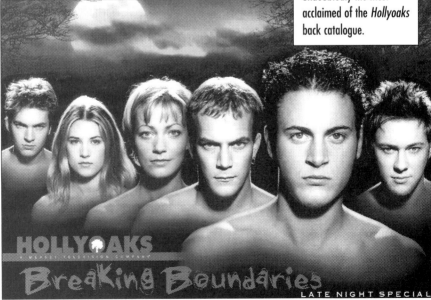

bullying campaign by Mark Gibbs (Colin Parry). The previous year, Luke had injured Mark in a football game, ruining any chances Mark might have had to play football professionally. In revenge, Mark started a bullying campaign against Luke. *Breaking Boundaries* portrayed the horrific climax to this story. After Mark and his friends had beaten Luke in the changing room they proceeded to chase him around Chester. Mark finally caught up with him when Luke's car got stuck in the mud.

CLASSIC MOMENTS

Luke realized that he had no choice but to face Mark and, after a fight between the two boys, Mark decided to teach Luke a lesson that he'd never forget and raped him over the bonnet of his car.

Playing alongside this shocking story was an insight into the tumultuous, yet ultimately passionate relationship of Lewis (Ben Hull) and Ruth (Terri Dwyer), and a comical depiction of Max Cunningham's (Matt Littler) first-ever sexual experience with Chloe 'the moose' Bruce (Mikyla Dodd). Despite these other stories, all eyes were on the devastated Luke as he struggled to comprehend what had just happened to him.

Breaking Boundaries was a defiant step forward for *Hollyoaks* in depicting a crime that had been regarded as such a taboo subject that no other show had dared to tackle it. After this episode, male rape ceased to be a literally 'unspeakable' crime and was finally accepted as one that did actually exist – a crime that most certainly needed a voice. Many support organizations now use this episode when counselling rape victims and the *Hollyoaks* researcher has had countless letters from victims who said that Luke's rape had given them the courage finally to confront what had happened to them.

It was something Luke would never get over, but as the months went by and Mark Gibbs was eventually sentenced, he began to put his life back together. *Breaking Boundaries* was an exceptional episode on all counts, from the skilful direction and superb scripting to the performances of the actors involved. Gary Lucy's performance in this episode was unforgettable and was duly recognized in awards ceremonies throughout 2000. Praise should also go to Colin Parry for a brave and chilling performance as his attacker, Mark Gibbs.

SERIES PRODUCER JO HALLOWS

Jo Hallows took time out of her busy schedule to direct this special episode and had this to say about the shoot: 'The coldest shoot ever and the longest hours, but undoubtedly the best results. The cast and crew were absolutely fantastic. We were outside on a Saturday night at 4am with snow and sleet, but that didn't stop some truly fantastic performances. Thankfully, these were duly recognized.'

psychological assessment. Ruth discovers she's pregnant and Finn finds out Victoria is Tony's mother. Luke tries to talk to his parents but bottles out. Ruth and Lewis take over the running of The Dog whilst Jack and Jill go away to try and save their marriage. Meanwhile, Sol befriends a young prostitute called Jess, but ends up being attacked up by her pimp. Finally, Tony's house is ready, but his plans to become a student landlord are scuppered when Taylor does an exposé on him, calling him a slum landlord.

MAY 2000

Tony discovers Finn's affair with his mother and takes the news badly. Nikki continues to annoy her housemates and moves into Tony's house, much to Carol's annoyance! Luke is still wrestling with his terrible secret and messes up his A levels. Ruth admits to Carol that she doesn't want the baby. Jess returns to see Sol but he struggles to accept what she does for a living. Jill splits up with Jack after admitting that she had slept with Dave and moves out. Zara starts to see her psychiatrist and turns to Paul for support. Max and O.B. buy themselves a camper van and a desperate Luke ends up trying to drive his car into a wall. He finally confesses to Adam what happened to him and Adam breaks the news to their parents. Sean arrives back in Chester and Matt decides to try to get back Holly's money. Meanwhile, Ruth has an abortion without Lewis knowing and tells him that she has miscarried.

JUNE 2000

Nikki flirts with Sam and Luke finally tells Mandy that he was raped. Finn and Lewis decide to convert their warehouse into a nightclub and Lewis is devastated when he finds out about Ruth's abortion and ends up hitting her. Sam worries that Anna will find out about him spending the night with Nikki. Mark calls round to see Luke, prompting him finally to confess all to the police and Mark is eventually charged pending trial. Matt manages to get Holly's money back when he tricks Sean into buying a music sampler, which turns out to be a house brick! Geri finds out about Sam and Nikki, and when Sam texts Geri pleading for more time, he sends it to Anna by mistake. Max and O.B. celebrate the end of their exams with a trip to Glastonbury, but come back with scabies! Geri's mother, Jacqui, pays her a visit and helps Anna take revenge on Sam. Tony volunteers himself and Carol to do a parachute jump and Jill confesses to Jack that she has a brain tumour.

JULY 2000

The whole of the Cunningham household has scabies and Jack finally persuades Jill to move back into The Dog. Tony and Carol start training for the parachute jump, but Tony develops a fear of flying. Zara is being bullied at school because of what happened to Luke, and Ruth gets a first and decides to stay on at college to do a PhD. Gina and Sol struggle to come to terms with Jill's illness. Luke hears that his rape case will go to court and Zara creates a fictitious relationship with Paul to try to impress Steph. Geri, Alex and Anna move into Tony's house. Carol starts to feel self-conscious about her bust size, especially when she is cast as an urchin boy in a film being shot locally. At Mr C's suggestion, Helen and Cindy open an ironing shop, but Max ruins the launch! Jill agrees to go to America for treatment and Luke goes away to France with his mother.

AUGUST 2000

Sam struggles to find a place to live and sleeps in Tony's caravan. Carol tells a doctor that she wants a breast enlargement and starts a 'boob-o-meter' to try to raise the money for the operation. Jill returns from America and breaks the news to Sol and Gina that her condition is inoperable. Lewis continues to borrow money from Lorraine and Finn asks Victoria to marry him. Sam and Anna call a truce and Max is devastated when he fails his A levels, but lies to his dad that he's done very well. Tony's dad reacts badly to the news of his divorce and saws each of his and Victoria's belongings in half, including Tony's beloved caravan. Zara gets septicaemia from a henna tattoo and Mr Morgan reads her diary, discovering all about her 'affair' with Paul. A hunky firefighter, Ben Davies, arrives in Hollyoaks and Mandy and Cindy vie for his affections. In a confrontation with Paul about Zara, Mr Morgan ends up injuring Paul's hand.

SEPTEMBER 2000

Jill tries to reconcile Gina and Emily, who are warring, but Emily has other problems when she ends up kissing Nikki. Thanks to crossed wires, Cindy and Mandy each think they are going out on a date with Ben, but he eventually opts for Cindy. Mandy tells Mr C about Max's A level results and Max dashes off in his camper van announcing that he's heading for France. Lorraine offers Lewis the chance of wiping out his debt – if he sleeps with her… New fresher Izzy Cornwell arrives in Chester and nearly drowns in the swimming pool, but is saved by Adam. Carol sells Beryl at an auction and Geri takes an instant dislike to Izzy, especially when she makes a move on Adam! A journalist turns up at the Morgans', hoping for an exclusive on Luke's story, and we bid farewell to Sam and Nikki, who decide to make a fresh start away from Chester, leaving a heartbroken Anna behind. The Loft finally opens and Carol marks the occasion by singing and is spotted by a talent scout.

OCTOBER 2000

At the last minute, Carol pulls out of her breast operation and decides to go and sing on a cruise ship. Sol and Gina take Jill to Blackpool, and Mr C and Chloe go in pursuit of Max and O.B. Jill sadly passes away, leaving Sol and Gina devastated. Geri discovers she has a stalker and Lorraine shows Lewis that she means business when she trashes his flat. Lewis takes advantage of the burglary and steals more items to sell himself and to top up his insurance claim. Lorraine decides to play an active role in the running of the club and Lewis has no choice but to confess to Finn that he owes her money. Finn uses the money Victoria put into the business to pay Lorraine back. Luke finally faces Mark in court and after four tense days, is relieved when Mark is found guilty. Cindy has problems when she has to take Holly to work at The Loft as Holly swallows an ecstasy tablet and has to be taken to hospital. Cindy is investigated by social services and she decides that she has no choice but to flee the country. In her mad dash to the airport with Ben in Tony's car, Cindy knocks Anna down. Ruth discovers that Lewis has lied about how much was stolen from the flat. He tells her about his debts to Lorraine and, in a rage, Ruth hits him and he hits her back. Luke sells the story of his rape to the papers for £20,000.

NOVEMBER 2000

Everyone is shocked by the news about Anna's accident and a hungover Tony finds himself under suspicion when he can't remember how either he or his car got home. Ben confesses to the Cunninghams that Cindy has left the country and Luke decides to move out and get his own flat. Tony is in the clear when he is hypnotized and remembers where he had been at the time. The relationship between Lewis and Ruth is still strained, but Ruth finally softens when Lewis agrees to attend Gamblers Anonymous. Ben confesses to his dad, Will, that he had been in the car with Cindy when it hit Anna, and Jacqui gets herself a job at The Dog. Geri is forced to move out to the caravan when Tony's new tenant, Laura, arrives. Sol discovers that Jess has been arrested and has been using Gina's name. He decides to help her get off the streets. Finn confesses to Victoria that he used her money to pay off Lorraine and they put Lewis on a wage until he pays them back. Meanwhile, Lewis continues to argue with Ruth and turns to Lorraine for comfort…

DECEMBER 2000

Sol is worried about Jess after her pimp forces her to return to the streets. Tony is smitten with new girl Laura. Luke is shocked to discover that his dad has been getting hate mail for not standing by him and Max and O.B. try to donate sperm. Luke finds a friend in Ben and Lorraine offers to help Lewis organize Finn's stag night. Ruth accompanies Lewis to Gamblers Anonymous and the boys all head to Barcelona for Finn's stag night (see page 78). Lewis panics that Lorraine is going to tell Ruth about their affair and so he confesses all, leaving Ruth heartbroken. Luke finally makes up with his dad and Zara has problems with her mother's mood swings caused by her dependency on tranquillizers. Finn marries Victoria, and Alex begins to realize that he has feelings for Anna, but is sidetracked when he discovers that he is infertile. Sol finally tracks down Jess and is shocked when she confesses that her pimp, Steve, is actually her brother! Sol moves Jess into the safety of The Dog, incurring the wrath of Steve, who takes revenge by setting fire to the pub on New Year's Eve.

JANUARY 2001

Ruth discovers the fire at The Dog and Jack is alarmed to find out that Sol and Jess are inside. Ben manages to rescue them, but Jess runs away, fearful of the repercussions. Laura steals the cloakroom money from The Loft, but feels guilty and returns it. Anna confides in Geri about Alex's infertility and is furious when Geri tells everyone. Meanwhile, Jess visits Sol in the hospital, only to be dragged away by Steve. Ben begins to develop feelings for Mandy, but is torn when Luke admits that he wants Mandy back. Theo arrives in Hollyoaks and quickly becomes Finn's sparring partner. Lewis steals from The Loft to fuel his gambling habit and when Finn notices money is gone, he sacks Laura. Zara's problems disappear when she falls for local Goth, Brian. Gina agrees to help Sol find Jess, but finds herself in trouble when Steve discovers she has been following him. Jack is suspicious about Lewis and Ruth's break-up and hints to Helen that he thinks Lewis might have hit Ruth. Max and O.B. borrow a sampler and record 'Get Down With That Thing'.

FEBRUARY 2001

Alex is having difficulty coming to terms with his infertility and takes his anger out on Anna for telling Geri. Max and O.B. convince Izzy to let them perform at The Loft, but their performance is a disaster. Mandy wants Ben to tell Luke

O.B., Mr C and Max perform 'Get Down With That Thing' at The Loft.

about their relationship but he never seems to find the right time. Sol is still desperate to track down Jess and The Dog finally reopens for business. Adam decides to do a *Big Brother*-style film for college by hiding cameras in Tony's house. Meanwhile, Alex hears Chloe on the radio, making jokes about infertility and assumes she's having a dig at him. He exacts revenge by having a one-night stand with her and dumping her the next morning. Mrs Morgan unwittingly shoplifts and Adam and Mr Morgan start to believe Zara's story about Mrs Morgan's addiction to tranquillizers. Sol trashes the car of one of Jess's clients and Steve decides to teach him a lesson by kidnapping Gina. He eventually lets Gina go, prompting Jess to finally go to the police and Steve is promptly arrested. Geri finds out about Adam's film project and uses it to her advantage. Alex decides to get a snake to prove his masculinity and Mandy develops a website for new models.

MARCH 2001

Zara and her mother call a truce and Geri continues to have fun manipulating Adam's film project. Luke invests in Mandy's business and they become partners and Zara makes the discovery that Brian is a Christian! Luke finds out that Mandy and Ben have been seeing each other behind his back and is devastated. Sol and Jess get a surprise visit from Steve and, after a scuffle, Jess accidentally pushes Steve off The Loft's fire escape. Lewis's gambling debts continue to spiral and, in a moment of madness, he almost hits his mother. This jolts him into going away to Ireland for a while to sort himself out. Tony implements a recycling system in his house and the students have problems at college when their lecturer is sacked. Jess is convinced the police will arrest her and things get worse when Steve regains consciousness and threatens to incriminate Sol. Sol and Jess are desperate, knowing that one of them will be blamed for Steve's fall. Tony's tenants are horrified to discover that Adam has been filming them and are further incensed when they find out that Geri knew about it. Tony takes drastic action by burning all the footage and unwittingly sets fire to his caravan and to Monty the snake! Luke asks the elusive Laura out on a date.

APRIL 2001

Tony encourages the students to eat a high-fibre diet after learning that the more waste his new system collects, the more money he gets! In a bid to make herself more alluring to Brian, Zara decides she wants to be christened and asks Ben to be godfather. Zara's plans prompt Helen into christening Tom, and Tony is honoured to be godfather. Problems at college continue when Taylor discovers that the sacked teacher had received a pay-off and organizes a sit-in at the college. It's a success but an obsessive Taylor reaches breaking point and refuses to let the students leave. Sol and Jess decide they have no choice but to flee the country, leaving a heartbroken Gina behind. Gina's bad luck continues when she discovers that Emily has been seeing another girl. Meanwhile, Alex's dad arrives to patch things up with his son, and Anna is shocked to discover that he's gay. Alex refuses to speak to his dad, but finally begins to realize how unkind he's been to Anna. Dan Hunter arrives in Hollyoaks and immediately has a run-in with lecturer John Stuart over parking. Dan's younger sister, Lisa, joins Zara and friends at Hollyoaks Comprehensive. Tony discovers that, as a result of his recycling system, he is drinking his own urine but decides not to tell the students. Anna finally accepts Alex's apology for his behaviour and they finally get together.

MAY 2001

Geri and Izzy decide to organize a games event to help raise money for the college newspaper. Gina becomes interested in raising money for a Chinese orphanage and decides to leave Chester to work for them. Tony's tenants find out about the recycling system and take revenge by tying Tony up and pelting him with sponges of his 'special' water! Lewis returns from Ireland a new man, his flash clothes and apparent wealth arousing Victoria's suspicions. Lisa is desperate to go on a school trip and is humiliated when her dad, Les, arrives and drags her off the bus. Meanwhile, Max discovers that O.B. has joined the drama society, which prompts him to sign up, too, bagging the main part. Finn worries that Victoria might be too old for him and, in a moment of madness, has a one-night stand. Tony is horrified when his septic tank explodes, covering his mother and causing his house to be condemned by the Environmental Health. Ruth is disturbed when she starts getting phone calls from a man wanting to speak to Kurt Benson and Anna is shocked to discover that she's pregnant. Meanwhile, Victoria has a scare when bricks fall from the roof of a building, but thankfully Lewis pulls her to safety.

JUNE 2001

Alex is adamant that he can't be the father of Anna's baby and Victoria's near-death experience is enough of a jolt for Finn to decide that he does love her after all. However, this happiness is short-lived when Lewis tells Victoria about Finn's one-night stand and brings Finn's marriage to an end. Mandy and Luke make plans for a fashion show at the college to advertise their website, and Mr Morgan decides he needs an image change and goes on a strict diet. A loan shark comes after Lewis and we discover that he took a loan out in Ireland using the name of Kurt Benson. Lewis is told that the loan must be repaid within thirty days. Geri's Giants and Izzy's Invincibles compete against each other in Game 4 IT, with Geri's team securing the victory. Ruth finds herself attracted to her colleague, John Stuart, and Geri gets together with Lewis. Luke and Ben finally make up and Alex discovers that the hospital made a mistake and he is fertile after all. He apologizes to Anna, but is adamant that he doesn't want the baby. A desperate Lewis tries to get hold of as much money as he can and ends up stealing the takings from Game 4 IT.

JULY 2001

Mr C stands for the Council and is riled when Tony stands against him. Lewis, still desperate for cash, sells Geri's car whilst she's on holiday. Zara takes advantage of Tony's house and throws a party, but the evening ends with her discovering Brian in bed with Steph. The fashion show causes countless problems for Mandy and Luke, especially when the models walk out and Mandy has to enlist the students' help. Mandy's mood isn't helped by an impromptu kiss between Ben and Laura on the catwalk. Anna goes for a scan and decides that she couldn't possibly have an abortion. Meanwhile, Izzy sets her sights on Dan, and Geri returns from her holiday with the news that she is now dating City striker Jason Cunliffe. Tony is excited to hear that Carol is coming home, and Mandy and Ben break up. Alex offers Anna money to pay for an abortion. Finn is given the unenviable task of telling Tony that Carol isn't actually coming back and the two old enemies finally call a truce. We meet Sally Hunter when she returns from another trip abroad – what has she been doing? Helen lends Lewis money on condition that he seeks counselling. Meanwhile, Geri goes to her first premiere on Jason's arm and Tony proudly unveils his garden biosphere.

AUGUST 2001

Matt decides to use Tony's new biosphere to grow cannabis. Zara and Brian finally reconcile as do Mandy and Ben, but Mandy refuses to accept Ben's conditions of just a casual relationship. The smear campaign between Mr C and Tony continues, but Mr C eventually wins his seat as councillor. Anna decides to tell her parents that she is pregnant. Ruth continues to date John Stuart, but is beginning to think that she'd be better off single, especially when she discovers that he has a young daughter. Tony quits his job in Deva to sell organic vegetables in the Yard and both Geri and Izzy are duped into lending Lewis money to pay off his ever-mounting debts. Mr C organizes a charity fête but the day ends in disaster when Tony mistakenly puts cannabis in the food. Lewis discovers Geri is two-timing him with Jason and tries to blackmail him. Ruth catches Lewis trying to set fire to The Loft and he finally confesses to her about the extent of his debts. Ruth persuades Tony and Finn to buy Lewis out of The Loft, thus severing all links with him. Tony and Finn decide to invest in a restaurant and Ruth decides to give up her PhD and follow suit. Les continues to keep Lisa on a tight rein.

SEPTEMBER 2001

Ruth, Finn and Tony move away from Hollyoaks Village to focus on Tony's new business venture, *Gnosh*. Zara is dismayed to find out that her mother is dating

Abby's dad, Will, and Theo gets a surprise when his younger brother Norman arrives. Alex returns to Chester and is furious with Anna for not having an abortion. Meanwhile, Mandy and Ben split up again and Abby and Zara become suspicious when Lisa refuses to go swimming – why is she trying to cover up marks on her arms? Tony and Mr C hold interviews for new tenants to their student properties and the new tenants are Eve, Jamie, Becca, Jodie and Nick. Jason makes a pass at Izzy, but is caught by Geri, who promptly throws him out. The two old enemies call a truce, but Geri ends up getting back with Jason. Jamie grows tired of Tony's house rules and moves in with his old friend Adam. Izzy is forced to sack Max from the college play and O.B. takes over as lead. Max then poisons O.B. and is called back to replace him. Luke and Mandy win a website award and find themselves getting closer, and Izzy begins to suspect that Dan might be taking drugs. Jamie starts dating Becca and Eve at the same time, and Luke and Mandy end up kissing. See *Movin' On* on page 66.

OCTOBER 2001

Mandy finally passes her driving test but not before a mad dash to the test centre when, unbeknown to her, Laura has hidden her keys. Luke and Mandy finally get back together but the relationship is brought to a premature end when Mandy discovers that Lewis has tried to kill himself. Nick is the victim of a street attack and Mandy makes the shocking discovery that Lewis has hit Ruth and she is unable to forgive him before he dies. As the Cunninghams mourn Lewis's death we are introduced to Bombhead, an old friend of Lee's, who is semi-naked in the schoolyard after selling his trousers. Helen asks Tony to perform the eulogy at Lewis's funeral and Mandy despairs at her mother's attitude to Lewis's death. As Helen and Mandy drift further apart, Laura steps in and helps Helen through her grief. Izzy confides in Adam about her suspicions about Dan, and Adam and Dan end up fighting, leaving Adam humiliated when he discovers that Dan is a diabetic. Jason gets groin strain and goes away with Geri to a specialist clinic, and Dan's friend Toby arrives. The Hunters' secret is finally revealed when we learn all about Ellie and how she went missing on a holiday in Ibiza. Lisa struggles to gain any freedom from Les and ends up running away from home when he refuses to let her sing at Brian's gig.

NOVEMBER 2001

The Hunter family are alarmed when Lisa disappears and their worries are exacerbated when Sally finds a blood-stained shirt. Alex gets together with Becca and Lisa finally returns home, but refuses to open up about her problems. Mandy continues to argue with Helen about Lewis and, in her confused state, ends up kissing Max. Brian begins to suspect that Les is beating Lisa and as Lisa's problems get out of control, her self-harming is revealed. Max asks Finn to tell him about Lewis's problems, and Beth Morgan returns from France.

LEWIS'S SUICIDE

Written by Neil Jones and Chris Parker
Directed by Anya Camilleri and Chris Johnston
Broadcast October 2001

Hollyoaks: Movin' On climaxed with the shocking, yet tragically inevitable, suicide of Lewis Richardson (Ben Hull). After years of trying to escape from his abusive father's shadow, Lewis began to realize that he was just like him, and drew the conclusion that there was nothing he could do to change himself. After two months of pent-up frustration, Lewis decided that the only way to make Ruth admit she loved him, was to beat a declaration out of her. The belief that he'd killed her, coupled with his feelings of complete desperation and alienation, led Lewis to take an overdose of pills. Even more tragically, Lewis was unaware of what he'd done the following morning, and it wasn't until Finn took him to the hospital the next evening that he realized that he had inflicted irrevocable damage to his liver. A week later, Lewis died in hospital, leaving behind a devastated mother, a bewildered sister and three angry, but strangely relieved friends.

> **DID YOU KNOW...?**
>
> Three different doctors had an input into the scripts detailing Lewis's suicide. *Hollyoaks* had a responsibility to ensure that this horrific storyline was told as accurately as possible.

With an outstanding performance from Ben Hull as the tortured Lewis, the character's agonizing death was one of the most horrific scenes in *Hollyoaks*'s history. The late-night slot also meant that the producers were able to demonstrate the full physical horror of Lewis's unbearable decline as his organs began to shut down. Not only did Lewis's story provide a dramatic climax to *Hollyoaks: Movin' On*, it also drew to an end Ruth's feelings of entrapment and suffocation. Ultimately, Lewis's death meant that she was free of him, and made her realize that it was time to move on. Ruth left *Hollyoaks: Movin' On* a new person, never to return to Hollyoaks. Lewis's death also had a profound impact on Tony and Finn and, although the shadow of his death still hung over them, they returned to Hollyoaks stronger than when they left. Lewis's death also kick-started another story, which continued in *Hollyoaks* for several months after

> **DID YOU KNOW...?**
>
> The make-up department spent several hours a day ensuring that Lewis's make-up looked authentic. Ben Hull even had to wear yellow contact lenses to show the full extent of Lewis's shocking liver damage.

Hollyoaks: Movin' On drew to a close. It focussed on the fallout for Lewis's family – would Helen ever get over her son's death? And would Mandy ever be able to forgive Lewis for what he had done? Even to this day, Mandy struggles to understand how the one man who had protected her against her father could ever have hurt another woman.

Meanwhile, Izzy tries to help find Ellie, and Brian and Abby decide to alert Social Services about Lisa – resulting in Social Services paying the Hunters a visit. Max has an electric shock while on a bonding fishing trip with Mr C, and Geri is jubilant when Jason scores the winning goal in an international game. Mandy realizes that she has no future with Luke, and Lisa self-harms when she learns that Brian doesn't fancy her. Lee walks in on her and, out of desperation to keep her secret, Lisa tells Lee that she'll run away if he tells anyone. In the special video release, *Hollyoaks: Indecent Behaviour*, Geri sees Jason in his true colours and Beth is raped by the footballer Scott Anderson. Geri decides to take revenge on Jason by marrying him and taking him for every penny.

DECEMBER 2001

Beth is in turmoil after the rape and finds an unlikely confidante in Geri, who tells her what went on between her and Jason on that fateful night. Max makes a play for Jodie, but they never quite get it together. Beth confides in Luke about her rape, but is sure she can cope. Sally returns from another futile search for Ellie with Gary in tow, the boyfriend with whom Ellie went on holiday all that time ago. Meanwhile, Luke decides to work in a football camp in Canada and warns Mandy to be wary of Laura. Les and Dan go over to Spain to identify a body and are relieved to find it isn't Ellie's. Meanwhile, the pressure gets too much for Lee and he tells Gary about Lisa's self-harming. Their relief is short-lived when Gary tells the family about Lisa's self-harming. Helen decides she wants to adopt Anna's baby, against the advice of Mr C and Max. The Hunter family struggle to understand Lisa's condition and Geri finally marries Jason. Their marriage is only fleeting as Geri throws Jason out of the car and bids farewell to Hollyoaks. Anna goes into premature labour and Max and Alex keep a vigil at her bedside. The Cunninghams, Morgans and Hunters all have a tense Christmas, with the Cunninghams' dinner climaxing in Helen hitting Mr C, and the Morgans' ruined by a sobbing Zara, who had been dumped by Brian for Lisa. The Hunters resolve to move on and put Ellie in the past. This is cut short by the arrival of a late Christmas card from Ellie. Finn organizes a New Year's party where a self-destructive Mandy gets drunk and goes home with Jamie.

JANUARY 2002

The New Year begins with a horrific car crash involving Mandy and Adam when Mandy drives her car off the road. Adam is seriously injured, and whilst the Morgans hope he will make a full recovery, Adam is told he may never walk again. Mandy starts the rumour that the Hunters must be to blame for the accident, following their service on her car and this has a rapid impact on their business. After seeing his baby, Alex is finally convinced that he wants to keep him and decides to apply for Parental Responsibility. However, Anna refuses to accept the child and tells Alex that she wants nothing to do with it. Beth enlists the help of journalist Alyson to help her incriminate Scott for her rape. After going to the press with her story, Beth has no choice but to break the news to her parents. Meanwhile, Chloe stands for Student President and Jamie promptly stands against her and a vicious election campaign ensues. Jamie eventually wins the title and Chloe takes the knock badly and begins to question her own self-image. Mandy is shocked to learn that the Hunters weren't to blame for the crash and she is charged with driving without due care and attention and must retake her test. Finn begins to question his role in life and decides that he needs some excitement. He promptly appoints Gary as manager of The Loft and sails off into the great blue yonder with a mystery woman. Beth's case finally gets to court and after a tense day, Scott is found not guilty of rape after the judge learns that Beth had coaching for her trial. Alex is granted Parental Responsibility of baby Charlie and Anna realizes that she has no choice but to try and make things work…

FEBRUARY 2002

Beth is determined to exact revenge on Scott, Anna struggles to adapt to life as a mother, and Chloe continues to have problems with her weight, which are compounded when she doesn't get the job as barmaid at The Dog. A shady customer called Ronnie asks Dan to do some illegal work on cars and Mandy struggles to cope with a baby in the student's house and decides to move back home. Mandy finally reconciles with her mother and they vow not to let Lewis come between them. Tony and Gary compete for power at The Loft and Jamie decides to organize a charity event to help Adam. Meanwhile, Alex is determined to make Anna see sense and learn to love Charlie, and Adam becomes friendly with Olympic diver Neil, who helps Adam confront his fears about his injury. Eve treats the football team to some of her holistic therapies, with disastrous results when the boys react badly. Brian discovers that Lisa is still self-harming and struggles to understand *why* she can't stop herself. Chloe's confidence continues to diminish and she ends up tearing up photos of her and Matt, upset at the way she looks. Ellie Hunter arrives back in Chester and visits Dan, hoping that he can pave the way for her return. Ellie eventually returns home but begins to realize the impact her absence has had on the family. Jamie hosts 'Splash 4 Cash', an event which angers Adam as he resents the college thinking of him as a charity case…

MARCH 2002

Gary finds out Ellie has returned and demands to know where she's been for two years. Dan and Ellie argue, with Dan unable to understand Ellie's flippant attitude to her absence. Nick goes on his first date with Greg, whilst Max opens up a burger van in the Yard. Chloe's image problems finally get to her and she breaks up with Matt, unaware that he was about to ask her to marry him. Anna

Lisa turns her problems on herself.

finally agrees to keep Charlie, and Alex and Anna take tentative steps towards life as a family. Jealous of Mandy's growing closeness to her mother, Laura announces that her mother is terminally ill and is the centre of attention once more. A self-destructive Beth finds herself turning to O.B. for support but after they spend the night together O.B. is upset that Beth doesn't want more. Tony takes Mandy out on a driving lesson, but Mandy struggles to gain confidence. Ellie learns about Lisa's self-harming. Laura continues her pretence and accepts Helen's offer of a ferry ticket back to Ireland, but doesn't board the ship. Beth takes matters into her own hands and visits Scott at the training ground. She ends up spitting at him and is arrested. Patty Cornwell arrives to visit her daughter Izzy and the female students head for a tranquil weekend at Jodie's cottage. However, the boys gatecrash and during the weekend the barn catches fire, but Nick manages to save the day. Laura makes the announcement that her mother has died and Steph decides to make a play for Scott.

APRIL 2002

Steph seduces Scott, much to Beth's disgust. Ronnie continues to offer Dan *dodgy* business at the garage. The stress of dealing with Ronnie, coupled with his fighting with Ellie, causes Dan to collapse and slip into a diabetic coma. Eve struggles to balance her finances and takes out several store cards in a naïve attempt to sort them. Izzy is shocked that her mother has got together with Jack and Adam decides to cut off his hair in a defiant effort to take his rehabilitation seriously. Tired of the constant arguments, Ellie decides to move out of home and moves in with Gary on the barge. Adam shows his lecturer a film he's been making of his rehabilitation and is upset when he's told that it's self-indulgent and that he should defer his degree. Mandy finds Laura overbearing and a desperate Beth vandalizes Scott's home. Meanwhile, Abby and Lee decide they want to lose their virginity but are rudely interrupted when Lee discovers Bombhead hidden in the wardrobe. Izzy finds a friend in Tony and Max is suspicious of Laura's behaviour and questions whether her mother actually *did* die. Adam and Mandy resolve their differences and Becca makes the shocking discovery that she has gonorrhoea. Becca assumes Jamie is to blame and he is subjected to a witch-hunt at the college. Steph begins to worry she's pregnant by Scott, but it's a false alarm. Brian walks in on Lisa cutting herself and is repulsed. In a desperate attempt to understand what she is going through, Brian tries to cut himself but faints at the sight of his blood. As a result of a one-night stand with Jamie, Ellie goes for a test and discovers that she too has gonorrhoea. She immediately warns Toby and we discover that Toby had had contact with Ellie whilst she was away and that they had slept together. Financial problems get the better of Theo and he has to close down Theologic and open a market stall, and Scott becomes smitten with Izzy.

MAY 2002

Charlie is christened, although tempers are frayed when Alex's dad arrives and Alex refuses to speak to him. Izzy is shocked to discover that Scott has followed her to a club and he tries to make her see his side of the story. Beth comes to Izzy's rescue and when she sees Izzy in distress, Beth tries to scare Scott and drives towards him, unwittingly knocking him down. Beth is arrested, charged with attempted murder and held in custody. Brian tells Les that Lisa is still self-harming and Les takes matters into his own hands by removing all the doors in the house. Mandy solves the gonorrhoea mystery and discovers that Ellie is the carrier. The residents of Chester turn against Beth for injuring Scott and ruining any chances he had to play in the World Cup. Izzy discovers that her father had been having an affair, but is determined to save her parent's marriage and eventually persuades Patty to return home. Adam offers to help Mandy with her business, making Laura jealous in the process. Lisa continues to rely on Brian and he turns to Zara for support and ends up kissing her. Jamie decides that he wants Becca back and a fellow prison inmate attacks Beth. Brian confesses to Zara that Lisa is self-harming and Zara resolves to make friends with Lisa. Mr C gets a letter from Buckingham Palace informing him that the Queen may be visiting Chester as part of her Golden Jubilee celebrations and as a result, he decides to put up Nick and Jodie's rent. Adam discovers a genuine talent when he becomes a radio DJ at the college and his confidence is bolstered when a caller asks him out on a date. In revenge for Dan telling Les about her having gonorrhoea, Ellie tells Les all about Dan's dodgy dealings with Ronnie. She drops another bombshell when she reveals to Gary and Dan that Toby knew of her whereabouts whilst she was away. Mr C receives another letter telling him that the Queen will be making a visit to Hollyoaks Village and would Mr C like to be her personal guide. Meanwhile, Adam's confidence takes a knock when his blind date walks out on him.

A LITTLE BIT OF JUNE 2002...

Mr C's Golden Jubilee festivities all go horribly wrong when he discovers that he's been set up by Nick and Jodie and the Queen had never intended to come to Hollyoaks Village. Abby and Lee finally consummate their relationship and Mr C takes drastic action by evicting Nick and Jodie. Toby becomes interested in Mandy and Becca finally takes Jamie back....

In 2001, *Hollyoaks* spawned its first ever spin-off series, *Hollyoaks: Movin' On.*

Following the success of the late-night episodes *Breaking Boundaries* and the Barcelona special, Channel 4 commissioned *Hollyoaks* to produce a sixteen-part, late-night drama. The idea behind the show was to cater for the audience who had grown up with the teenagers of *Hollyoaks* and were interested in how their lives would progress as twenty-somethings. The show was to be based around Ruth Osborne, Finn, Lewis Richardson and Tony Hutchinson, focussing on their lives as they left their teenage years behind and faced the worries and pressures of the adult world.

Phil Redmond described his original idea for the series: 'People tell me that they are getting "too old" – at twenty-two, scary isn't it? – for *Hollyoaks* and can't quite identify with the new, younger characters. At the same time they still want to know what will happen to the older characters like Finn, Tony, Ruth and Lewis once they move on from Hollyoaks… I thought it'd be interesting to follow the older characters as they move on.'

The initial storyline pursued in *Hollyoaks: Movin' On* was the decline of Lewis Richardson, who since splitting up with Ruth had turned to heavy drinking and gambling. The characters moved to another part of Chester where Tony had bought a restaurant, *Dick Tasties* (later renamed *Gnosh* by Tony – 'good food, served posh'). Ruth followed, desperate to leave both Hollyoaks and Lewis behind her, and with Ruth came Finn, disillusioned after his failed marriage to Tony's mother. Lewis, meanwhile, followed Ruth, desperate for her to give him one last chance. It was this that would ultimately lead him to make the terrible decision to kill himself.

Hollyoaks Village was replaced by Northgate Mews, and, whilst the four characters continued to pop back in and out of Hollyoaks, over the next two months their lives were to change dramatically. Leaving behind the familiar faces of Hollyoaks, Ruth and the gang were soon to become embroiled in the lives of a brand new collection of misfits.

Two of the new characters, Sam and Louise, shared a flat above the café. Sam (Sarah Manners) was an old school friend of Ruth's. She was a happy, carefree girl, who viewed work only as a means to an end and devoted most of her time and energy to guaranteeing that she would always have a good night out. Sam worked in various temping jobs throughout the series, most of which began and ended on the same day due to her refusal to take work seriously. Towards the end of the series, though, she found a job that she loved – working for a record company – but unfortunately, she was unable to persuade them that she was worth taking seriously. Sam belonged to a close-knit family, and yet she had no interest in settling down – her philosophy in life being to live for the moment. Sam was the complete antithesis to her flatmate, clothes-shop manageress, Louise (Abigail Fisher). Louise was an emotionally vulnerable girl, who spent the majority of her time scrutinizing life

and analysing every situation she found herself in. She was a voracious reader of self-help books, due mainly to the fact that she had cared for her alcoholic father, Bob, since her mother died in a car accident. Louise had had to grow up too soon, and was keen to settle down in order to find the stability that she'd never had. She found love in her work colleague, Ritchie, but lost him to her supposed friend, Tara. She found a soulmate in Lewis, but after a while, even she found his self-destructive behaviour too much to contend with. Louise was life's proverbial doormat, who seemed destined never to find any sort of happiness. In the attic flat above the girls, lived Vic (Mark Cronfield), an assistant chef in Tony's new restaurant and an oddball who caused Tony no end of problems. Vic had been raised by the Salvation Army, and had then trained as an undertaker, leading a very isolated existence. He had a simplistic attitude to life and very rarely ventured out of Northgate Mews. His one companion was his scraggy, old dog, Cynthia, who was in fact a male, but, as Vic explained, 'She doesn't know that!'

Hollyoaks: Movin' On proved a significant success for Mersey Television, securing regular audiences of one and a half million over its eight-week run. Whether or not we return to Northgate Mews is still unknown. If we ever do, there will be a significant audience waiting with baited breath to discover whether Sam will get back with record company boss Paul; whether Vic will change his life now he's a landowner, and whether Louise will ever be lucky in love.

The Review

Student Elections

It's been another hectic year at Hollyoaks Community College with the student elections providing the most outspoken opinions of this academic year. The election of Student Union President usually comes and goes without the bat of an eyelid. This year was different – the heavily publicized campaign between first year Jamie Nash and second year Chloe Bruce had the whole college divided and provided one of the closest and entertaining political slanging matches of recent years. (Of course, nothing tops Taylor James's occupation of the Media Lab, but that's old news!) Of course, *The Review* doesn't condone bringing personal politics into campaigns, but the slanging match between Chloe Bruce and Jamie Nash regarding policies (with Chloe's argument that Jamie didn't have one) culminated in a rather cruel personal attack on Chloe's (dare we say it?) rather voluptuous figure. Chloe is indeed a favourite of *The Review* for her commitment to Hollyoaks FM, yet we can't help but agree that Jamie Nash's campaign provided some much-needed entertainment to what is usually a rather lacklustre event. Chloe offered protests on student grants and Jamie offered free beer every Thursday. Unsurprisingly, Jamie won by a landslide. Whether or not he was the right man for the job remains to be seen. However, one thing is certain: we at *The Review* can't help but raise a toast to Jamie on Thursday nights at the Union. Social gratification aside, we will have to wait to see if Jamie can provide as much commitment to the welfare of the students, as he does to the abundance of first years seen leaving his presidential flat (thanks for that tip, Anonymous).

'He who laughs last...'

Chloe Bruce may have lost out on the student elections, yet she may very well be uttering the expression, 'hubris' when asked to comment on the recent fall from grace of Student Union president Jamie Nash. It was a moment that every student dreads, it seemed that there was an outbreak of a Sexually Transmitted Infection. Every student who'd found themselves enjoying a quick fumble under the Union pool table made a quick dash to the local clinic and those afflicted hung their

heads in shame whilst trying desperately to construct a list of possible perpetrators. Just as the furore was dying down, the story took a rather bizarre twist when whispers began to circulate that the perpetrator was none other than our SU president, Mr Jamie Nash. Chloe Bruce was quick to jump on the bandwagon and before long, petitions and posters began to spring up around the college attacking our president on a level of which unseen since Beckham kicked Diego Simeone in the 1998 World Cup.

The Changeling

It was billed as the event of the year, yet few could have anticipated the disappointment that was the drama society's version of *The Changeling*. The play had attracted considerable attention from the male population, principally because the delectable Izzy Cornwell was to play the female lead of Isabella. The part of Alonzo was due to be played by Sam O'Brien, but at the last minute and with no explanation (though we reckon it was nerves), he pulled out. Max Cunningham stepped in to play the lead, but unfortunately he couldn't save what was most certainly one of the most lifeless, soulless and wretched versions of Thomas Middleton's classic. Miss Cornwell's performance was leaden and awkward, and as for Max Cunningham, words cannot even begin to express how bad he was. Having said that I'll have a go – his performance ranged from terrible in parts to shocking in others, ghastly at the beginning of Act One and dire at the close of Act Two. This play was due to run for a week in the college hall. Unsurprisingly, the curtain came down after the first night.

Chester Fashion Week

Another event attracting a fair amount of excitement amongst the male population of Hollyoaks Community College was the fashion show organized by former *Riverbank Review* 'Babe of the Month', Mandy Richardson! She was assisted by Luke Morgan, who was himself the object of unwelcome press attention back in 2000. The show was billed as a 'fashion spectacular', where outfits designed by Jed would be shown off by some of the most beautiful girls in Chester. All looked good for us until Luke Morgan scared off all the models when he told them that they'd be wearing fur! Of course, the boring protestors reared their ugly heads, even though Mandy was quick to point out that they would, in fact, be wearing *fake* fur. Suddenly the dream of models in the college was snatched away from us, until the game (and, dare I say it, gorgeous) Geri Hudson (now Cunliffe, but that's another story…) offered to step in and we all breathed a huge sigh of relief. The sigh grew to a cheer, when it was announced that Izzy Cornwell had also agreed to model. Just when we thought the evening couldn't get any better, a catfight broke out between the two girls. The perfect end to a beautiful night. God bless, Geri Hudson.

The Review has always had a reputation for its cutting-edge journalism and, in celebration of this, we take a trip down memory lane and pull out a few articles from our bygone years that encapsulate the life and times of Hollyoaks Community College. The first article from the archive was written by the late Ollie Benson.

Chips for Sex *by Ollie Benson*

Ever been in the canteen, boys, and wondered why you seem to have less chips on your plate than the girl in front of you? Then wrack your brains no longer; the answer is about to be revealed to all those of us left hungry in the afternoon and wondering why.

After several months of careful observation and assessment, I can finally reveal that canteen assistant Lee Robert Stanley is dispensing more chips to girls than he is to us boys! I know Stan personally, and can exclusively reveal that this underhand technique is quite simply a ploy to try and seduce these unsuspecting girls. It is most certainly a blatant misuse of college supplies and resources and should be stopped immediately. To all those girls who have been subjected to Stan's excessive helpings of chips – don't submit to his charms and remember that there are plenty of guys out there who, whilst not being able to offer extra chips, should at least be given a chance.

A classic article from former deputy editor of *The Riverbank Review*, Ollie Benson. Ollie left an indelible mark in *The Review* and, during his life on the newspaper, he introduced such seminal articles as, 'Wimp of the Week', 'Cleavage of the Year' and 'Babe of the Month'.

Ruth Osborne

Another graduate of *The Riverbank Review* and later *The Review*, former editor Ruth Osborne, is now a freelance journalist living in London. She left Chester in October 2001, and is already beginning to carve out a successful career in journalism.

Gina Patrick

Another memorable contributor to *The Review* is Gina Patrick. Gina played a major role in college politics with former partner Emily Taylor. Gina is now in China as a voluntary worker in an orphanage. She recently sent us the following email: *Having a great time in China, work very rewarding and I've made some great new friends. Miss everyone in Chester. Hope to see you all again soon, Gina XX*

TONY HUTCHINSON *played by Nick Pickard*

A stalwart from episode one, Tony Hutchinson, alias Nick Pickard, has appeared in almost 800 episodes of the show! From humble beginnings as an assistant chef in Riverbank College canteen to business entrepreneur with a nightclub, a restaurant and a student house to his name, Tony has had an extraordinary seven years. He has loved and lost more times than any other character in the show – including Julie, Tess, Jasmine, Lucy, Carol, Ruth and now even Izzy – and yet his enthusiasm and zest for life continues as always. Whilst often ridiculed for his middle-aged sensibilities and his romantic attachment to his wallet, Tony has repeatedly proved his worth as a friend to Kurt, Jambo, Finn, Lewis and most recently Mandy, whom Tony helped come to terms with her grief for Lewis. Whether Tony will find true love is difficult to say, yet underneath that buffoon-like exterior, there is a sensitive, loving guy just waiting for the right girl to come along.

Name: Nick Pickard

Age: 26

Place of Birth: Chertsey

Earliest Memory: Running up some stairs

Favourite Film: *The Shawshank Redemption*

Favourite Band: Jamiroquai

Ideal Woman: Jennifer Aniston

Favourite holiday destination: Hawaii

Who would you want to play you in a film of your life: Hugh Grant

What three things would you take with you to a desert island: A football, a TV, and alcohol!

What have been your highlights from the early days?

Probably the marriage episode. The show had been nominated at the National Television Awards and they showed the clip of me being jilted at the altar by Julie and showed people like David Jason laughing at my clip where I shouted, 'She's turned me down, *she's* turned me down!' It was just a great episode – my mum is never someone to make a fuss, but she phoned up after that episode and said it was brilliant. It was the fact that we were all dressed up in morning suits for this wedding that wasn't to be. I've still got the picture in my house of us all outside the church.

When do you think the producers found the comedy in Tony?

I think it started with my wardrobe; it was so bad and so straight away I knew Tony was a bit of a plum. I just started pulling a few funny faces and it all started to follow. It was pretty obvious with the stuff Tony went on about that he was too old for his time.

Ben (Marcus Patric)

Dan (Andrew McNair)

Carol (Natalie Casey)

Becca (Ali Bastian)

bottom left: Anna (Lisa Kay)
bottom right: Alex (Martino Lazzeri)

Front row (left to right): Jude (Davinia Taylor), Ruth (Terri Dwyer); back row (left to right): Dawn (Lisa Williamson), Lucy (Kerrie Taylor), Maddie (Yasmin Bannerman).

Geri (Joanna Taylor)

Izzy (Elize du Toit)

Front row (left to right):
Stan (Nathan Valente),
Ollie (Paul Leyshon),
Bazz (Toby Sawyer);
back row (left to right):
Jambo (Will Mellor), Kurt
(Jeremy Edwards), Tony (Nick
Pickard), Lewis (Ben Hull).

Jambo (Will Mellor)

$w^2 = (12g/a)[N_0/(1+3N_0^2)].\sin\phi$

A Tumbling Toast Falls Butter Side Down

Finn (James Redmond)

Mandy (Sarah Dunn)

Kurt (Jeremy Edwards)

Jamie (Stefan Booth)

Ellie (Sarah Baxendale)

Lee (Alex Carter)

Tony (Nick Pickard)

Front row (left to right): Mandy (Sarah Dunn), Helen (Kathryn George), Cindy (Stephanie Waring), Lucy (Kerrie Taylor), Mrs Benson (Martine Brown), Carol (Natalie Casey), Ty (Gary Grant); second row (left to right): Ruth (Terri Dwyer), Lewis (Ben Hull), Gina (Dannielle Brent), Luke (Gary Lucy), Adam (David Brown), Jasmine (Elly Fairman); back row (left to right): Jack (James McKenna), Sol (Paul Danan), Jill (Lynda Rooke), Tony (Nick Pickard), Paul (Zander Ward), Wayne (James Corden).

Lisa (Gemma Atkinson)

Abby (Helen Noble)

Steph (Carley Stenson)

Zara (Kelly Greenwood)

Lewis (Ben Hull)

Opposite
Front row (left to right):
Alex (Martino Lazzeri), Geri
(Joanna Taylor); back row
(left to right): Nikki (Wendy
Glenn), Sam (Tim Downie),
Anna (Lisa Kay).

Laura (Lesley Johnston)

Ruth (Terri Dwyer)

O.B. (Darren Jeffries)

Adam (David Brown)

Max (Matt Littler)

Chloe (Mikyla Dodd)

(left to right): Jamie (Stefan Booth), Gary (Guy Leith), Jodie (Kate McEnery), Nick (Darren Bransford), Izzy (Elize du Toit), O.B. (Darren Jeffries), Ellie (Sarah Baxendale), Ben (Marcus Patric), Becca (Ali Bastian).

Luke (Gary Lucy)

What have been your most memorable episodes?

Ibiza was great, especially with Tony coming back with crabs! I had the best scene of my life in Ibiza – Jo Hallows had organized a line of girls, all of whom had to get into bed with me, take off their tops and snog me. I said afterwards that that would have to be the best thing I've ever done. The ones I didn't want to kiss, I just gave Jo the nod... I loved the parachute story as well, because I got to do the jump. However, when it came to actually making the jump, I had to do my dialogue and then wait and all that time I was just looking out at the drop. There was a point where I nearly didn't go, but I did... I remember that the watertank episodes were long and hard. We were treading water for five hours a day and by the end of it we were knackered.

DID YOU KNOW...?

Nick Pickard has an impressive CV. Prior to *Hollyoaks*, he was in Steven Spielberg's *Empire of the Sun* and played the lead in the film, *The Land of Faraway*.

If circumstances had been different, who do you think Tony would have ended up with – Lucy or Carol?

It would probably have been Carol – they had such a love/hate relationship, it was a real case of opposites attract. I loved working with the girls and miss them both. Kerrie Taylor was just the most professional actress there will ever be, and Natalie would come onto set, not even looking at her script and would be magic.

What direction do you see Tony heading in?

I've never been one to come up and ask about my storylines because half the fun is in not knowing. It would be nice to get Tony a girl, but then the running joke seems to be that Tony can't keep hold of one! Unless Tony's character changes, no girl would want to be with him. He's getting a bit better now, but that's probably because he hasn't got any friends! Whatever happens to him, I really do still love playing Tony; I still get a real buzz doing what I do.

JAMBO, JUNE 1998

Played by Will Mellor
October 1995–June 1998

James 'Jambo' Bolton was undoubtedly one of the most unconventional and memorable characters ever seen in *Hollyoaks*. Jambo was an individualist, putting his unique stamp on anything that came his way – from his formula for salty vinegar, to his devotion to Margaret the cow. Jambo had a penchant for climbing through windows, yet, as he argued, 'Why walk round to the door when the window is right in front of you?' The irrepressible Jambo finally bid farewell to Chester to begin a new life in Anglesey in 1998.

Jambo was good friends with Kurt and Tony and, whilst they were often confused by his odd behaviour, the three formed a strong bond, providing one another with the support and, very often, humour needed to get through their rather tumultuous lives. Whilst Kurt was soon paired off with Ruth and Tony was hopelessly in love with Julie, Jambo was often left on the sidelines,

DID YOU KNOW...?

Jambo's cow Margaret was stolen by students whilst on location in Anglesey and they held her for ransom!

First seen: Climbing through Kurt's window to discuss plans to gatecrash Louise's party!

Last seen: In Anglesey, offering a shoulder for Lucy to cry on

Finest moment: Finally getting together with Dawn after two years of missed opportunities

Worst moment: Losing his beloved Dawn

Funniest moment: Stealing Margaret the cow, and his debut as 'Jazzo the Clown'

Love of his life: Dawn Cunningham

Most embarrassing moment: His unwilling debut as a stripper at Parkers when Jill Patrick grabbed his clothes

Most likely to say: 'What if…?' – Jambo was constantly in pursuit of the answers to those little mysteries in life

Least likely to say: Anything conventional – Jambo embraced the surreal in life and refused to adhere to any sort of convention

Place most likely to have been seen: At the garden centre, at the Bensons' hoping to be fed or climbing through the window of The Dog!

Hobbies/Interests: Trying to achieve that one invention that would change mankind as we know it, such as the luminous lollipop stick!

unlucky in love and unable to act on the feelings he had for Dawn Cunningham. After countless missed opportunities as well as Jambo's brief relationship with Carol's sister, Anita and his stepmother Lisa, Dawn and Jambo finally admitted their feelings for each other and millions of viewers breathed an enormous sigh of relief when they got together at last. The other woman in Jambo's life was his Bond Bug *Beryl*, whom he loved and cherished almost as much as Dawn! Tragically, Jambo's romance with Dawn was short-lived, as she was diagnosed with leukaemia. She eventually lost her battle against the disease, leaving Jambo devastated over the loss of the girl he'd wanted more than anything else in the world.

Jambo never got over the death of Dawn and, although he tried to persevere with his new landscaping business, 'Dig It!', he decided that there were too many memories of Dawn in Chester and that he wanted to move on. However, Jambo certainly left the female population of *Hollyoaks* with a memory they would cherish, when he was the unwilling stripper at Jude's opening night at Parkers!

Jambo made one final visit to Chester to put flowers on Dawn's grave and vowed never to return. We saw Jambo again when the gang went on a trip to Anglesey to visit him. As they left Jambo in Wales, it was clear that *Hollyoaks* would never be quite the same without him.

MANDY RICHARDSON *played by Sarah Dunn*

Our second-longest serving character, Mandy Richardson, arrived in Hollyoaks in October 1996. She was the under-age temptress of Ollie Benson and dreamed of becoming a supermodel. However, her world was turned upside down when it was revealed that her father had sexually and physically abused her. Thanks to the support of her older brother, Lewis, Mandy found the strength to take a stand against her father and he was sentenced to seven years in prison. Mandy's life slowly returned to normal and she got together with Luke Morgan, beginning one of the most popular love stories in Hollyoaks. Tragically this relationship was brought to a sharp end when Luke was the victim of a vicious sex attack. Mandy briefly found solace in Darren Osborne and then later in Ben Davies, yet her devotion and affection was always for

Name: Sarah Dunn

Age: 20

Place of Birth: Billinge

Earliest Memory: The first time I counted to 100 when I was about 4!

Favourite Film: Bridget Jones's Diary

Favourite Band: Coldplay

Ideal Man: Brad Pitt

Favourite holiday destination: Mauritius

Who would you want to play you in a film of your life: Julie Andrews when she was younger!

What three things would you take with you to a desert island: A mobile phone, a lifetime supply of Dairylea and a toothbrush!

Luke. She helped him get over his rape ordeal, but her own life was once again turned upside down when her brother, and protector, Lewis, committed suicide. This drove a wedge between Mandy and her mother, Helen, and she started to use Laura as a confidante, continually oblivious to Laura's, at times, odd behaviour. Mandy has since reconciled with her mother, runs a successful business and, after a brief dalliance with Jamie, has settled on Toby Mills. But in the tumultuous world of Mandy Richardson, nothing seems to last for long...

What was Mandy's first big story?

My first big story was with Paul Leyshon [Ollie] and Nathan Valente [Stan]. We had lots of party scenes and the underage sex story was my first big story-line. The rape storyline was the next big one.

How did it feel to be the centre of such a big storyline?

I saw things happening in the scripts and thought that it was a bit weird and the character of my dad started drinking heavily. I then found out what was actually going to happen – they asked me if I was all right doing it because I was only fifteen at the time. They had to ask my mum as well, because she still came with me at the time. It was just brilliant to know that, one, I was staying on and two, that I got to do something that was so controversial which I could sink my teeth into and be able to research.

What was the impact of Mandy's story?

I had a few letters telling me how good they thought it was and how believable it seemed. The actor that played my father, David McAlister, was an excellent actor. He was so believable that I was genuinely scared in the scenes. He would be vicious and grab hold of me, and all the fear from me would be real! Apparently people used to boo David on the streets, but he was a really nice man – just a convincing actor.

Why do you think Luke and Mandy were so popular with the audience?

Luke was so popular because he was such a nice boy and everyone felt sorry for him. At the time, Mandy was finally in control and everything was going well for her and I think it was a nice combination. They were the classic teenagers in love – everyone watching was like, 'I want a boyfriend like that', or 'I want a girlfriend like that'.

Who else would you have liked to have played in *Hollyoaks*?

I think I would have liked to have played Jude and been the cow! She was really feisty and didn't let anyone mess her about.

What direction would you like Mandy to go in?

She needs a stable boyfriend now that Luke's gone. I'd like to see her business becoming successful, because at the moment it's happening but it's not quite there yet. Things keep setting it back and Laura's being a bit odd. For once, I'd like Mandy to be in control of every situation she finds herself in.

IBIZA

Written by Roy Boulter
Directed by Jo Hallows
Broadcast 23 and 26 September 1996

After a summer break of just over two months, *Hollyoaks* came back in spectacular fashion with a two-part special, featuring the boys in Ibiza. After months of planning, Kurt, Jambo, Bazz and Tony finally got away to Ibiza. Kurt, on a break from Ruth, was keen to experience some Spanish delicacies; Jambo was too, although his heart, as always, was in Chester with Dawn. In contrast, Tony wasn't on the look-out for any girl – he'd just had his heart broken by Julie and was still in a period of mourning. Bazz, on the other hand, was more concerned with getting his and Kurt's record played, but kept disappearing at night, leaving the rest of the boys confused by his absence.

As always, *Hollyoaks* delivered the goods, treating us to two sun-soaked episodes in Ibiza. The episodes stand out for two reasons – firstly because these were the first episodes of *Hollyoaks* to be shot on location abroad; secondly they marked the dramatic and spectacular renaissance of Tony, who arrived in Ibiza as a clumsy and self-conscious assistant chef and returned as a super-stud, after getting together with fourteen girls! In a complete reversal of fortune, Jambo and Kurt left with no notches whatsoever on their bedposts. Tony left with the unreserved respect of Jambo and Kurt, but their envy soon dissolved when Tony discovered that he had contracted crabs during his escapades, and began panicking about how he would explain it to Julie!

Bazz was driven throughout the holiday by the ambition to get one of the clubs to play his record. He did manage to get an impromptu play, although it was out of the speakers of a local bus that he had 'borrowed'. Inevitably, Bazz found himself in trouble with the police, but luckily, Maria, Tony's latest conquest, had connections with the Spanish police (her father!) and Bazz was released without charge. There was still the mystery of where Bazz was disappearing to in the evenings, a fact which suggested that Bazz was somehow not really one of the boys. It would come to light much later that this disappearing act was provoked by Bazz's confusion about his sexuality, but it would be a few more months before anyone realized this.

Ibiza was undoubtedly the perfect backdrop to the new era of *Hollyoaks*. It had returned as a fully fledged, twice-weekly

soap, and there could have been no better way to bring it back after a summer break. The four boys returned to Chester and, within a year, one had been jilted at the altar, one was married, one was grieving the death of his girlfriend and one had realized that he was gay. This snapshot episode was symbolic of happier times, before the boys were faced with impending adulthood and all of the traumas and responsibilities that would go with it. Ibiza was a time for pure, unadulterated fun – growing up could wait for two weeks!

BARCELONA
Written by Allan Swift
Directed by Peter Rose
Broadcast 11 December 2000

In the spirit of the Ibiza episode, in December 2000 *Hollyoaks* took the boys to Barcelona. What followed was an explosive combination of romance, action, sex and, of course, the inevitable explosion. Like *Hollyoaks: Off on One*, this was again *Hollyoaks* with a touch of Hollywood, as the boys went on an unforgettable stag weekend

DID YOU KNOW...?

Hollyoaks has been a hit around the world and has been shown in fifteen countries across the globe: – Sweden, Norway, Netherlands, New Zealand, Thailand, Denmark, Indonesia, Romania, Iceland, Belgium, Greece, Poland, Spain, Israel and Turkey!

to celebrate Finn's forth-coming marriage to Tony's mother, Victoria.

The boys were hoping for the usual things from the weekend – sun, sea, sex and drink – yet, with the exception of Max, everyone spent most of the two days in pursuit or being pursued by a collection of odd characters. Alex was chased by an angry transvestite by the name of Nemesis, who had stolen his money belt; Luke, Ben and Sol were pursued by the locals, thanks to Sol's inability to blend in with Spanish culture; O.B., on the other hand, found himself in a compromising position with a glamorous older woman, only to find out that she was Alex's transvestite, Nemesis!

Lewis's problems with Lorraine continued when she arrived unannounced and, after showing him compromising photographs of the two of them, bribed him into helping her snatch her son, who lived with his father in Barcelona. After snatching the boy and being chased across Barcelona, Lorraine was finally forced to return her son to his father. She blamed Lewis for this and swore to reap her revenge.

The stag had a far from relaxing trip when he discovered that Tony had enlisted the help of Carol to persuade him not to marry Victoria. After Finn very nearly succumbed to Carol, he decided that Victoria was indeed the woman he wanted and resisted temptation. In a fit of rage, Tony took revenge on Finn by firing an arrow at his backside! It was whilst Finn was being examined by doctors that Carol and Tony began to realize that they had feelings for each other. They threw caution to the wind, hoping to put their disastrous night in Newquay behind them for good.

Finn and Tony left Barcelona with a new understanding. Tony was now convinced that Finn did genuinely love his mother, and he also realized that Carol was the girl he had always wanted – but would she come back to him? Alex and O.B. both returned to Chester with guilty secrets of their experiences with the transvestite, and Luke and Ben had had enough of Sol to last them a lifetime. The only person to return with any good memories was Max, who spent a night of passion with the beautiful Diti and finally put paid to the rumour about him being 'three-seconds Max'!

Although the boys pledged to keep loyal to 'the law of the stag' and never reveal what happened in Barcelona, you can still catch the odd embarrassed glance between O.B. and Alex, as Tony and Max continue to this day to remind them of their escapades with the transvestite, Nemesis.

GORDON CUNNINGHAM *played by Bernard Latham*

Gordon Hilton Cunningham first arrived on our screens in March 1996, providing comfort for his daughter Dawn as she struggled to fend off the advances of her mother's new boyfriend, the creepy Terry. Mr C soon became established in the show as he tried to help his first wife Angela overcome crippling debts, and tried to inject some discipline into the lives of his wayward children. He soon built up a witty repartee with Tony when Mr C became landlord of Got It Taped and found himself in various scrapes in his desperate attempts to keep Max and Cindy on the straight and narrow. Mr C lost his beloved daughter, Dawn, in December 1997 and was saddened when Jude ran off a year later after getting herself in trouble with the police. Mr C rediscovered the joys of romance later in life, falling for the recently divorced Helen Richardson. When he discovered that she was pregnant with his child, he did the honourable thing and offered to marry her. With Helen came Mandy and Lewis, prompting the merging of the Cunningham and Richardson familes. With the Richardson family came considerable angst, culminating in Lewis's death, yet Mr C has proved himself to be a rock to his wife, Helen, and their son, Tom.

Name: Bernard Latham

Age: 50

Place of Birth: Manchester

Earliest Memory: Singing to the passengers every day on the old red bus taking me to nursery

Favourite Film: *Seven Samurai*

Favourite Band: The Beatles

Ideal Woman: My wife

Favourite holiday destination: Greece

Who would you want to play you in a film of your life: Matt Littler

What three things would you take with you to a desert island: The Complete Works of Shakespeare, a widescreen digital TV and a large bottle of sunblock

Why do you think Mr C is such a cult figure?

I've had a few young people coming up to me saying, 'I wish you were my dad'. I think it's because I go on a level with Matt [Max] when we mess about and I have a bit of fun. I'm also a bit of a buffoon, but in times of strife I can actually pull it together, so he's more like a middle-aged everyman.

When do you think the producers discovered Mr C as a comic figure?

I think it was in the sixth episode – I was only due to be in six. By the time the sixth episode came around, I thought that if I want to stay in the series, I can't be shouting all the time and being serious. I'll get invited back if I can actually inject some humour into the show. So I started playing a little softer and tried to show that Mr C could go other places than just being a grumpy old father who had deserted his children.

What's been your favourite storyline?

When I accidentally took marijuana at the music festival – that was a nice little storyline. Becoming a councillor, all those kind of things… Even the Morris dancing, basically just being silly. In contrast, I enjoyed the opportunity to work on the Lewis storyline which I thought was a really good and responsible story.

What's been your favourite episode with Matt Littler?

Basically, nearly every episode with Matt because we work really well together. I remember the driving lessons I gave him because it was like the son off the old block, because we were combatting Mandy because she was useless and Max passed first time. We've worked together for so long that we have this rhythm going, so we know what each other does. It's easy to work with someone like Matt because he's very open.

Who do you miss from the old days?

I would say Davinia Taylor – she was very gifted. She was a wild child but she was the one that you used to fight with most on set, not literally – you used to have to fight to get the scene back off her because she'd steal almost every scene she was in. I don't think she realized how good she was. And Lisa Williamson, who played Dawn, she was a lovely, lovely lady.

What's next for Mr C?

I tell you what I'd love to do – I would love to get involved with the villain of the piece. I would like Mr C to run him over, kill him and then get done for it, but ultimately get away with it!

DID YOU KNOW...?

As well as *Hollyoaks,* Bernard Latham can also be seen in the films *Erik the Viking* and *The Rainbow.*

JUDE CUNNINGHAM, DECEMBER 1998

Played by Davinia Taylor
March 1996–December 1998

Jude Cunningham was almost certainly one of the most self-centred, vibrant and daring characters ever seen in the show. She led a colourful life, battling with drink and crippling debts. Jude seemed to be never short of luck, and yet invariably something always seemed to go wrong for her. However, she struggled on, regardless, desperate to make her fortune and live happily ever after.

Jude began life in *Hollyoaks* studying fashion at Riverbank College, but her academic life was short-lived, as she was thrown off her course for cheating. After this, she struggled to make ends meet and, due to her irresponsible attitude towards money, was declared bankrupt and left with massive debts to clear. As Jude became increasingly desperate for money, she began working as an escort, but finally gave it up after a few bad experiences with clients. Just as Jude began to get her life back together, tragedy struck when her sister, Dawn, lost her battle against leukaemia. Jude took the news badly, turning to

First seen: Arriving home in Chester after Natasha's death

Last seen: Saying goodbye to Cindy, with Dawn's passport and wearing a black wig, preparing to flee the country

Finest moment: Offering to donate her bone marrow to her sister, Dawn

Worst moment: Losing Dawn to leukaemia

Funniest moment: Discovering Max and O.B. were stowed away in the back of her van and were drinking the wine

Love of her life: Lewis Richardson, though her lies destroyed their relationship

Most embarrassing moment: Giving out leaflets in the local precinct, dressed as a bunny girl!

Most likely to say: 'Why me?' – Jude's plans often backfired on her, continually getting her into trouble

Least likely to say: 'I want to settle down...' Jude loved taking risks, thriving on the excitement of it all

Place most likely to have been seen: Working at Parkers, or at car salesrooms asking for test rides

Hobbies/Interests: Fashion and making as much money as possible

drink to get her through the difficult times. The love of Jude's life was Lewis Richardson, but she lost him when he grew tired of her lies.

When Mr C's shady cousin, Benny, arrived on the scene, Jude soon hooked up with him and started stealing cars to order. As she finally managed to pay off her debts, she bought into Parkers and it seemed as if life was starting to get better for her. As always, this was short-lived for Jude, as she struggled to repay Benny what she owed him. Things turned nasty when Benny trashed Parkers and, to cover her losses, Jude began doing illegal booze trips to France. However, this still didn't bring in enough money for the final instalment to buy her beloved Parkers. Desperate to make a success of her business, Jude agreed to do one last job for Benny. She had to pretend to get married, so that Benny could snatch an expensive piece of jewellery stored at a stately home. Unsurprisingly, the heist went wrong and Jude was left as the number one suspect. She was days away from being arrested by the police and had to come up with a plan quickly.

A desperate Jude had no choice but to leave Hollyoaks. She bought a dark wig, took Dawn's passport and bid a sad farewell to her sister, Cindy. Despite Jude's selfishness and shady dealings, she has remained one of *Hollyoaks* most popular and enduring characters, whose relentless obsession with money was the ultimate cause of her downfall.

MAX CUNNINGHAM *played by Matt Littler*

As a character, Max Cunningham has been in the show since November 1995. Matt Littler took over the part in September 1997 and since then Max has provided a little light relief for Hollyoaks, most often with his friends O.B. and Sash. Like Mandy, Max has seen his fair share of tragedy, with his sister, Dawn, dying from leukaemia, Jude and Cindy fleeing the country and later his stepbrother, Lewis, committing suicide. Despite all of this, Max has managed to retain his humour and, whilst he refrained from going down the college route with O.B., Max is still keen to make his first million. He has remained close to his father, often the source of some classic comedy moments – for example, the day Mr C took Max fishing and failed to notice that Max had got an electric shock from an overhead wire! Max has revealed his sensitive side in his affection for Anna, helping her during the difficult stages of her pregnancy. He seems to have met his ideal girl in Jodie Nash, but something always seems to get in their way. Max is now a successful entrepreneur with his burger van firmly established in the Yard. Now all he needs is a girl to make his life complete.

Name: Matt Littler

Age: 20

Place of Birth: Bolton

Earliest Memory: A birthday party – sitting on a window-sill

Favourite Film: Couldn't say – I love films

Favourite Band: Stevie Wonder

Ideal Woman: Kirsten Dunst

Favourite holiday destination: Jamaica

Who would you want to play you in a film of your life: Me or Darren Jeffries

What three things would you take with you to a desert island: My three best mates

How did you get into acting?
When I was four we did the nativity play at primary school. It wasn't a traditional nativity – we did *The Lion and the Mouse* and I ended up playing the lion and just fell in love with it there and then. I then started to go to a before-school and after-school drama club, and then drama school at the weekends and then ended up going to the Oldham Theatre Workshop.

The part of Max was played by someone else originally (Ben Sherriff). What was it like to take on someone else's character?
I didn't really watch it much, so it didn't really affect me. I'd watched it a couple of times because I knew Natalie Casey. Actually, I met Ben a few weeks ago and he's really involved in his music, so good for him.

You and Darren (O.B.) had to grow up on screen. How was that?

We saw an old episode the other day and it's weird! It's funny seeing how Max and O.B. have grown up. When we first started, boobs and women were funny, now Max and O.B. look at the world and find that funny. It's nice to see young people who don't have that many problems. They've got issues, but they prove that not everyone's messed up.

What has been your favourite storyline?

I remember nicking Jambo's car, *Beryl*, and thinking that was hilarious, we nicked *Beryl*'s ear [*Beryl* had ears attached to the roof] – it was proper *Reservoir Dogs* which was quite cool. Another favourite was when Max and O.B. stowed away to France, and obviously Barcelona was a great laugh!

Max and Mr C are most people's favourite comedy double act. Why do you think you work so well together?

I live with Bernie (Mr C), so at night sometimes we do a bit of rehearsing and stuff. Bernie's an old pro, so I learn a lot from him and he's always telling me when I'm doing something wrong.

When Lewis died, Max was involved in a particularly dramatic storyline. How did you find it?

It was fantastic. I was used to coming into work and just messing about as Max, suddenly I was coming in and saying some serious things. It was a great storyline to sink my teeth into, especially some of the stuff with Sarah [Mandy].

If you could play anyone else in *Hollyoaks*, who would it be?

Either baby Tom, because he only works one and a half hours a day – he just sleeps and doesn't get any lines... Or I would like to have played Rob Hawthorne; it would have been quality to have played a baddie.

Sam O'Brien
Hollyoaks Community College

Business Studies Coursework

'To produce a detailed account of a successful business entrepreneur – for example Bill Gates or Richard Branson. Within your account, you are to highlight strengths and weaknesses of your chosen entrepreneur, as well as detailing problems they have encountered on their road to success and how they have overcome them.'

I have chosen to examine the business career of successful Chester entrepreneur, Max Cunningham. I will examine his journey from humble beginnings as a vacuum cleaner salesman to successful burger-van entrepreneur. Although Max is a good friend of mine, I guarantee that the following analysis will be an impartial guide to his successes, as well as examining his less successful business schemes. I have personally been involved in some of his ventures, and I will attempt to highlight the strengths and shortcomings of each individual project.

May 2000 – Sandwich Salesman – Max's first successful business plan was an ingenious idea to sell home-made sandwiches in the local establishment, Drive 'N' Buy. Unfortunately, his business was nipped in the bud when the shop's owner, Mr C, discovered that he was taking all of his ingredients from the shop. Mr C reclaimed the money for the ingredients from Max's wages. However, the business had been initially successful and would set Max on the path that would eventually lead him to great success.

May 2000 – As live statues – Another idea of Max's was for me and him to become live statues in Chester city centre. This involved standing still for several hours, whilst people gave money after being amazed by our skills. Unfortunately, we incurred the wrath of several nearby 'statues' and were chased away. This was an important lesson in the necessity of researching and investigating potential competitors. It was a venture we decided not to try again.

July 2000 – The launch of a new business – In July, Max learnt a valuable lesson in the importance of a successful business launch. Max played an integral part in the opening of local business venture Steam Team. The local business entrepreneur, Helen Cunningham, had organized a steam-

roller as a novelty device to make the launch of her new ironing shop memorable. The launch was running smoothly until Max decided to have a go on the steamroller and accidentally crashed into his stepsister, Mandy Richardson, who was dressed as a giant cake. Admittedly, this was not one of Max's most successful moments in business.

September 2000 – Customer relations – In September 2000, Max and I got jobs in Blackpool organizing donkey rides along the beach. It was here that Max learnt a valuable lesson in the art of customer relations. In a moment of madness, Max likened one of the customers to one of the donkeys and unfortunately, we were both dismissed from our positions. In hindsight, this was a valuable lesson for Max and for me in the importance of building a good relationship with the customer base.

November 2000 – The importance of careful planning – Max learned another valuable lesson when he began working as a vacuum cleaner salesman. Max was keen to carve out a career as a salesman. Unfortunately, when he performed a practical demonstration at the house of local businessman Tony Hutchinson, Max failed to study the instructions on his cleaner carefully. He attempted to vacuum Tony's carpet, demonstrating along the way what stains his vacuum cleaner could eradicate. Max had misread the instructions, mistaking 'soil' for 'oil' and poured engine oil onto Tony's carpet. When Max tried to suck up the oil,

he made a giant hole in the carpet. Thankfully, Max quick-thinkingly cut a piece from beneath Tony's sofa to replace the damaged area. He never sold another vacuum cleaner, but was unperturbed – he was still determined to make his first million.

November 2000 – Painter and decorator – Max and I tried another business venture when we went into the painting and decorating business. We were employed to paint the flat of our mutual friend, Luke Morgan. Unfortunately, Max and I misinterpreted his instructions and painted his flat pink. After we had repainted the flat its intended colour, we decided that painting and decorating was not an affluent business into which we should venture.

December 2000 – Sperm donations – This was a valuable lesson in the importance of thorough research before entering into a business scheme. Max and I had overheard that the local hospital was willing to pay for people wishing to donate sperm. We were both quick to offer our services but were saddened to discover that we wouldn't be paid for what we had to offer.

December 2000 – A Christmas Grotto – This venture proved to be another lesson learned about sussing out direct competitors before attempting to go into business. Max, our friend Chloe Bruce and I decided to turn our camper van into a grotto. We planned to use Chloe as Mother Christmas and collect money for a local charity. Unfortunately, this incurred the wrath of a nearby Christmas grotto and a war developed between the two parties. This culminated in a fight within our own ranks, when Chloe discovered that the money we had been collecting might not have been destined for the local orphanage.

January–February 2001 – The record industry – This was, without a doubt, our most successful business venture to date. Max and I decided to record a dance track, which we hoped would reach the upper regions of the charts. We sampled a recording of Mr C shouting, 'Get down with that thing' and after some considerable tinkering, we recorded the track. Mr C was happy to come onboard – he paid for the pressing of 200 CDs and even agreed to make a personal appearance at The Loft to perform the track. Unfortunately, the general public were not as receptive as we had hoped and, although the track was a considerable underground hit, it never quite managed to propel us into the limelight.

May–September 2001 – The acting industry – Sadly, Max failed to learn his lesson with the failure of his record. In May 2001, he struck upon the idea of becoming a thespian, deciding that it was his destiny to tread the boards. After much coaching and squabbles within the ranks, he finally performed as the lead in *The Changeling*. Sadly, his performance was a disaster. Max once again learnt the harsh lesson that it is notoriously difficult to carve out a successful career in the entertainment industry.

March 2002 – A fully fledged entrepreneur – After almost two years of knock-backs, triumphs and failures, Max Cunningham finally found the business venture that would most certainly net him his first million. Max decided to use our old camper van to sell burgers from and, after much wrangling with local club owner, Tony Hutchinson, finally unveiled his burger van in the heart of Hollyoaks Village. Max knew his customer base well: he knew that there was a dire need for the product and, after his father pulled a few strings at the local council, he finally got a licence to trade. Already the van is doing a roaring trade and Max has finally proved that he does have the makings of a successful business entrepreneur. Watch this space, because in a few years' time, Max's burgers will be on every street corner. I am proud to say that I was a part of his considerable success story, and have learnt several valuable lessons along the way.

KURT BENSON, JANUARY 1999

Played by Jeremy Edwards
October 1995–January 1999

Cool, charming and with dashing good looks, Kurt Benson was undoubtedly the most popular and dynamic character ever seen in *Hollyoaks*. He was the embodiment of cool – living for his music and his motorbike, and devoting much of his time to securing the affections of the beautiful Ruth Osborne (Terri Dwyer). After a rocky start to their relationship, they ended up getting married. As a result, Kurt and Ruth became icons for all teenagers in love, demonstrating that love can conquer all.

Their decision to marry was provoked by the trouble Kurt had got himself into after injuring Spike. Kurt had caught Spike making a play for Ruth and, in his attempt to protect her, he pushed Spike, causing him to fall from the scaffolding. As a result, Kurt was accused of attempted murder and was certain that he would be found guilty. He took off to Hull, sensing that Ruth doubted his innocence. Ruth went in pursuit of him, however, and they decided to make the ultimate commitment to each other and got married, incurring the wrath of their parents when they returned home. When Kurt was found not

First seen: Printing off fake invitations to Louise's party

Last seen: Driving off on his motorbike, leaving a tearful Ruth behind

Finest moment: Taking revenge on Rob by leaving him in the middle of the sea

Worst moment: The death of his younger brother Ollie, and almost losing his sister Lucy to drugs

Funniest moment: His attempts to locate the 'Unidentified Bleeping Object'

Love of his life: Ruth Osborne, but they married too young

Most embarrassing moment: Failing his motorbike test when Tony stopped him in the middle of it to ask for advice about Julie!

Most likely to say: 'I hate Hawthorne' – Kurt made no secret of his relentless hatred of Rob, which began when Natasha died

Least likely to say: 'Ollie, what's mine is yours...' – Kurt spent most of his time trying to keep Ollie out of his room and away from his precious belongings

Place most likely to have been seen: Parkers or The Dog – academic work was never high on Kurt's list of priorities

Hobbies/Interests: Music – particularly the guitar – and his beloved motorbike

guilty, the couple began to enjoy life as newly-weds, although they knew that things would never be easy.

Another chapter in Kurt's life began when he handed Rob Hawthorne over to the mercy of his drug dealers, who threw him from the roof of a car park. Rob never forgave Kurt, and began a long and drawn-out plan to exact revenge. Rob's plan culminated in getting Lucy hooked on heroin and, when she fell into a drug-induced coma, Kurt took matters into his own hands and followed Rob to France. After a dramatic chase and confrontation, he left Rob floating in the middle of the Atlantic, announcing that fate would decide his destiny.

As Lucy slowly recovered from her ordeal, Kurt and Ruth's marriage hit a rocky patch and they both began to wonder whether they'd made a mistake marrying so young. Ruth was determined to make it work, but Kurt soon found himself tempted by the alluring Kate Patrick and started an affair. Ruth found out about Kurt's infidelity and threw him out, but he managed to persuade her that he'd made a terrible mistake and she eventually took him back.

Kurt's decision to leave was prompted by a violent outburst when he caught Kate trying to drown Ruth in the swimming pool. He tried to teach Kate a lesson by holding her head under water, and almost drowned her in the process. Ruth was shocked by his violent reaction – this was a Kurt she barely recognized. After much soul-searching, Ruth and Kurt decided to call it a day. 'I'm going to let everyone get on with the rest of their lives. I'm going to go away to grow up, so we can both work out what it is we really want...' Kurt said, and he left, promising Ruth that he would always be her friend. Tragically, just six months after saying goodbye, he was killed in a jet ski accident.

With the departure of Kurt, *Hollyoaks* lost its most iconic figure. The show will always have its hunks and heroes, with the likes of Dan Hunter and Ben Davies as the next generation of Kurt Bensons, yet Kurt was there right from the start, and he left an indelible mark on the show.

SAM O'BRIEN (O.B.) *played by Darren Jeffries*

Whilst we have yet to meet his own family, Sam O'Brien has become a surrogate member of the Cunningham family since his arrival back in October 1997. O.B., Sash and Max proved to be a troublesome trio, constantly in scrapes both at school and with the residents of Hollyoaks. Jambo was a long-established enemy of Max and O.B. when they stole his car Beryl and offered her for ransom. The boys were always on a scam to make money, often leading them to take desperate measures, such as stowing away to France in the back of Jude's van. O.B. finally lost his virginity with Chloe in the summer of 2000 and, after Max failed his A levels, they decided to up sticks and move to France. However, they only managed to get as far as Blackpool! O.B. returned to Chester, settled into life as a student and found

Name: Darren Jeffries

Age: 20

Place of Birth: Wrexham

Earliest Memory: Three years old, when my sister was brought home from hospital

Favourite Film: *Star Wars*

Favourite Band: Travis

Ideal Woman: Kirsten Dunst

Favourite holiday destination: I'd love to go to Australia

Who would you want to play you in a film of your life: Me – because I might need the work!

What three things would you take with you to a desert island: Music, food and my Playstation 2!

himself embroiled in various student activities. He became friends with Jamie Nash. Yet despite his college friends, he still shares a close bond with Max and they continue to offer each other support as they face the problems that come along with impending adulthood.

How did you get into acting?
I did a three-week drama course that I saw advertised in the paper. I wanted to learn more about acting. At the end of the course we did a play, and an agent came to see the play and she signed me up. A couple of weeks later I got my first audition, which was for *Hollyoaks*. I was fifteen when I first started.

What was it like growing up on screen?
It was weird; when we were younger we were the youngest ones on the cast because everyone else was over twenty. There were only me, Matt (Max) and Sarah Dunn (Mandy) who were under twenty. As we've grown older, our characters have as well. Now they're roughly the same age as everyone else on the show. Matt and I notice how Lee and Bombhead are having the stories that Max and O.B. would have had a few years ago.

What's been your favourite storyline so far?

The stuff I enjoyed doing the most was when O.B. and Max went over to France when they snuck in the back of Finn and Jude's van. It wasn't filmed in France – it was shot in Fleetwood – but it was the first time I'd ever done a big story out on location. I loved going to Barcelona – it was great having all the boys out there and having a laugh. I also loved the DJ storyline with Max and Mr C, when we recorded 'Get Down With That Thing' – we had a really good laugh and it lasted for a couple of weeks and had a beginning, middle and end. It was really well received; we had loads of people telling us how funny it was and shouting, 'Get Down With That Thing' at us!

Which cast member do you miss from the early days?

I still see quite a few of them. I see Will Mellor a lot. Natalie Casey was really cool; she was quite young when she started so she always had time for me and Matt.

O.B.'s quite a comic figure. Would you like to do a bit more drama?

I love doing the comedy because I think I'm better at it, but I've done loads of it since I started. I'm not bored of it, but I welcome new stuff. I'm enjoying O.B.'s drinking storyline at the moment because it's something different and it's a challenge as well, whereas when I'm doing the comedy, it sort of borders on doing it with your eyes closed – although I still enjoy doing it.

What next for O.B.?

I'd like to see O.B. get a girl-friend and sort himself out because he's a bit pathetic when it comes to women! I think he needs to sort himself out generally when it comes to women because whereas Max seems to have got it sussed, O.B.'s still not really sure. Any of the girls will do – anyone that would just make him happy and not treat him like an idiot.

Before our schedules were brimming with shows like *Popstars*, *Pop Idol* and *Soapstars*, *Hollyoaks* carried out a nationwide search for talent in 2000 (perhaps inspiring these later shows to follow in its footsteps!). *Hollyoaks* has always been built on the philosophy of producing new and exciting talent, and the statistics speak for themselves in the wealth of talented actors that have used *Hollyoaks* as a springboard to successful acting careers. Initially, the producers decided to hold open auditions in Manchester in March 2000 to source any as yet undiscovered acting talent for the show. Series Producer Jo Hallows explained at the time, '*Hollyoaks* is fast approaching its

Karl Dolan, a producer of *Hollyoaks* had the unenviable task of masterminding the auditions. Not only did he have to plan the logistics of the tour; he was also producing a documentary for Channel 4 to chronicle the auditions.

Why did you decide to do *On The Pull*?
We've always done open casting sessions at Mersey TV, but on a much smaller scale. The idea was to take this idea and turn it into a bigger event. Not only would it allow us to go out and find exciting new talent, it would be a great boost for the show to get out on the road and meet some of its viewers. Once we decided to do the auditions, it all came together so quickly. We had done an audition in Manchester, with no plans to take it further afield. We saw some great talent in Manchester, as well as attracting some considerable press exposure. Out of this came the idea that this was something we should do on a nationwide scale. To each venue we took existing cast members to offer advice to people waiting to be seen — we deliberately chose people who had been given their first big break by the show.

Would you ever consider doing *On The Pull II*?
There's nothing in the pipeline right now, but never say never! The four main characters we have in the show as a result of *On the Pull* are testimony to its success, so perhaps we should consider doing it all over again. Shows such as *Popstars* have taken the format and moved it on, so if we were to go out on the pull again it would be good to develop the concept even further.

What particular qualities were you looking for?
Each stage of the auditions allowed us to get a feel for someone's personality, as well as their ability to act. One of the most important considerations was to find people who would be able to work with the cameras and the people we pulled had the enthusiasm to learn this skill. What they looked like was a secondary considera- tion; the four people we pulled had a certain something that we knew would come across well on screen.

On The Pull attracted a fair amount of criticism from people who felt they weren't given long enough to audition. How do you feel about this?
The number of people who turned up at the auditions dictated the pace at which they had to be run. This was the only way to give everyone who took the trouble to turn out on the day an equal chance of being selected. A certain amount of bad publicity from an event of this scale is only to be expected. However, the good public- ity far outweighed the bad, with most coverage recognizing what we were doing by giving a fair chance to everyone who thought they might have what it takes to be in the show.

fifth year [in 2000] and we need to expand. We are looking to discover our next generation of raw, new talent.' It was the success of the open auditions in Manchester that gave *Hollyoaks* the idea of carrying out a nationwide tour of auditions. When 8,000 people turned up to audition at the Opera House, the producers began to realize how many young hopefuls there were out there wanting their big break and the idea for *On the Pull* was born...

The plan was to tour the country and allow budding performers from England, Ireland, Scotland and Wales the opportunity to audition in front of Casting Director Dorothy Andrew. In true *Popstars* style, Dorothy would select the people she felt might be right for the show and, as this list was whittled down further in workshops and readings, the final few would be called back on the second day to meet Jo Hallows. Jo and Dorothy would put

> **DID YOU KNOW...?**
>
> On average, **18%** of the *Hollyoaks* audience are under 16, **54%** of the audience are 16–34, **20%** of the audience are 35–54 and **9%** of the audience are over 55! More females watch the show than males with a ratio of 60:40

the actors through more auditions until they had drawn up a shortlist. These final few would then be called back to audition in Liverpool for Executive Producer Phil Redmond. It seemed a simple enough plan, yet the one factor that the producers underestimated was the sheer volume of people who would turn out for the auditions. The first *On The Pull* audition was held at the Channel 4 studios in Horseferry Road in London. The producers had anticipated that the event would attract a large crowd; yet few could have predicted that over 20,000 people would turn out, causing Central London to come to a standstill! The producers suddenly realized that this was going to be much bigger than they had ever anticipated.

THE *On The Pull* TOUR

London – *15 April 2000*

Although the massive turnout had not been anticipated, the producers saw every single person, albeit at a fast and furious pace. Two of the young hopefuls at that audition, Marcus Patric and Andrew Somerville, were lucky enough to be asked to audition in Liverpool. Within a matter of weeks, Marcus arrived on our screens playing trainee firefighter Ben Davies and by the end of the year, Andrew made his debut as the enigmatic Theo. The overwhelming success of this audition was reported in all the national newspapers the following week.

> **DID YOU KNOW...?**
>
> Cindy Cunningham, Darren Osborne, Max Cunningham, Beth Morgan, Jess Holt, Lorraine Wilson and Will Davies... have all been played by two different actors!

Edinburgh – *19 April 2000*

The auditions were held at The Hub in Edinburgh and over 5,000 people attended, with the queue stretching all the way down The Royal Mile. After auditioning a considerable amount of talent, the producers selected twenty-year-old History student, Elize du Toit, to come to Liverpool for further auditions. Within two months, Elize had started work on *Hollyoaks*, playing Izzy Cornwell.

Chester – *29 April 2000*

Hollyoaks returned to its spiritual home of Chester to audition over 8,000 young hopefuls from the North West.

Cardiff – *6 May 2000*

The tour moved on to Wales and auditions were held at Cardiff International Arena with over 5,000 people auditioning. Like Chester and Edinburgh before it, there was considerable talent on display and several young hopefuls were 'pulled' for further auditions in Liverpool.

Belfast – *21 May 2000*

Hollyoaks went over the water to Waterfront Hall in Belfast for the final stage of the *On The Pull* tour. Lesley Johnston was among the 5,000 young actors who auditioned and she was eventually offered the part of Laura Burns.

Belfast marked the end of the open auditions that had seen over *40,000* wannabe actors audition in front of the *Hollyoaks* team. Not only was it a unique opportunity for actors without any previous experience to audition, it allowed the producers to view a considerable amount of young talent. Jo Hallows explained at the time: 'Having toured the country from April, I am delighted with what we went out and found. We have discovered raw new talent, which will enrich an already talented cast.'

Whether or not *Hollyoaks* goes back on the road remains to be seen. The

four actors we pulled are still in the show today, and are testament to the success of the project. It is now difficult to imagine the show without Izzy, Ben, Theo and Laura. They have matured as performers and have fast become four of the most central characters in the show, yet just over two years ago they were standing in line alongside thousands of other young hopefuls. In time, *Hollyoaks* will need to find the next generation of Izzys and Bens. When this time comes, *Hollyoaks* will do its best to allow young hopefuls the opportunity to be part of this. Watch this space...

LAURA BURNS *played by Lesley Johnston*

Without a doubt one of the most elusive, enigmatic and odd characters ever seen in the show, the strange and secretive Laura arrived in Tony's house in November 2000 and soon found herself fending off Tony's advances. Laura struggled to finance her first year at college, reaching such desperate measures that she stole the cloakroom money from The Loft. She soon had a fit of conscience and owned up to what she'd done. Laura became friends with Mandy Richardson and we sensed that she was beginning to develop an unhealthy obsession with Mandy's life, which reached its peak when she started going out with Luke. After the relationship fizzled out, Laura continued to drive a wedge between Mandy and Luke, and seemed to enjoy the problems Mandy had when Lewis

Name: Lesley Alison Johnston

Age: 19

Place of Birth: Belfast

Earliest Memory: Sitting in my cot aged two, calling out for my sister

Favourite Film: *When a Man loves a Woman*

Favourite Band: U2

Ideal Man: My boyfriend!

Favourite holiday destination: I'd love to go to Fiji

Who would you want to play you in a film of your life: Me!

What three things would you take with you to a desert island: My boyfriend, a good book and some food

committed suicide. After Mandy and her mother became estranged, Laura filled the gap and enjoyed being part of the Cunningham family. As Laura continues to try and control Mandy, we are beginning to learn more and more about her family. As Laura finally begins to open up, it looks as though she is finding some sort of stability – but is it just a bluff?

What were you doing before *Hollyoaks*?

I was studying beauty therapy because I wanted to be a make-up artist. I was still living at home with my mum.

How did you find out about *On the Pull*?

I found out the night before the auditions from a friend of mine who worked in the same modelling agency as me. She asked me if I wanted to go along for a laugh, as there were a couple of people from our agency going and we could go along and take the mickey! So we went along but no one from our agency went apart from us!

Tell me about the audition.

We arrived at 8.30am and it was really cold outside. It started to rain and we had got all dolled up and had a little bit of a hangover from the night before. We queued for about two hours and the documentary crew asked me and my friend a few questions, so we thought that that was a good sign. I remember seeing Gary Lucy and Terri Dwyer walking across the car park and having a laugh. We met Dorothy Andrew [Casting Director] and had one minute to talk about ourselves. It took me about fifteen seconds to tell them my life story! I was asked to go through to the next stage. We then had to audition by reading from the scripts. Then at the end of the day they told me that they wanted me to come to Liverpool. I came to Liverpool and auditioned again, I was told I had the part and went back to Belfast. I then had to wait about three and a half months before I started filming!

Can you remember your first day on set?

My first scene was with Joanna Taylor [Geri] and Lisa Kay [Anna]. I had to twist Joanna Taylor's arm behind her back and on one of the takes I accidentally hurt her – so it wasn't a good start to my first day!

Laura's an elusive character – how would you describe her?

I think she's been alone for a lot of her life and she's scared of that. I play it as if there's a mental disorder there because I had studied psychology. It's difficult for even me to say who she is because I prefer to just get little bits of information when they're revealed in the script. It makes it more exciting for me to play.

What does the future hold for Laura?

It's difficult to say because there's so many different things you could do with Laura, anything we're going to do with the Mandy/Laura storyline will be fantastic. The next six months will be the hardest because it's when I'm going to find out the most about Laura and then it's my job to put that across on screen so everybody else understands it.

LUCY BENSON, JANUARY 2000

Played by Kerrie Taylor
October 1995–January 2000

During her time in *Hollyoaks*, Lucy Benson had more than her fair share of tragedies and heartache. She started off as Kurt's sensible and level-headed sister, but this soon changed when she hooked up with Rob Hawthorne. Little did Lucy know that her relationship with Rob would tear her family apart, put her own life in jeopardy, and cause her and her friends so many years of terror.

After being involved in the accident that caused the death of Dermot, Lucy soon wised up to Rob, and even shopped him to the police. It was Lucy and Kurt's role in seeking revenge that caused Rob to be thrown off a car park roof by his dealers. Unbeknown to Lucy and Kurt, this marked the beginning of his vendetta against the Bensons – an obsession that would continue throughout his life. With Rob well and truly out of her life, though, Lucy returned to normal – she started a band with Carol and Bazz and was happy that things seemed to be going her way. As is inevitable in *Hollyoaks*, happiness for Lucy was short-lived. Her life was turned upside down when her younger brother, Ollie, was killed in a car crash. Lucy blamed herself for the

---

First seen: Telling Kurt that the police wanted to talk to him about his 'stolen' car

Last seen: At the airport, bidding a sad farewell to Tony

Finest moment: Shopping drug dealer Ty to the police, to avenge the death of her friend Clare

Worst moment: Her heroin addiction, and the deaths of her brothers Ollie and Kurt

Funniest moment: On her double date with Carol, having to pretend that Kurt was her boyfriend!

Love of her life: Most probably Bazz, but she was devastated to find out about him seeing Matt behind her back

Most embarrassing moment: Having her father Kirk as the manager of The Crazy Bazz Studs

Most likely to say: Something clever – Lucy was extremely bright and was always armed with a barbed comment when Kurt or Ollie annoyed her

Least likely to say: 'No' – it was Lucy's inability to say 'no' to Rob Hawthorne that led her down the road of heroin addiction

Place most likely to have been seen: Parkers, gossiping with best friend, Carol

Hobbies/Interests: Music – Lucy was a keen drummer in both The Crazy Bazz Studs and later The Lewis Carol Experience

accident, as she had encouraged Kurt to chase after him. Lucy found it diffi-cult to get over Ollie's death, and ended up turning to Rob for support. He offered Lucy tranquillizers to get her through the difficult times. Once she was well and truly hooked on them, Rob upped the dosage to heroin and so began a downward spiral that would eventually put Lucy in a coma.

As Lucy finally weaned herself off heroin, she attempted to piece her life back together. However, Rob Hawthorne was to cause further trouble when he trapped Lucy, Lewis, Ruth and Tony in a watertank. They managed to free themselves, but afterwards Lucy lived in constant fear of Rob and what he would do next. She was finally freed from this worry when Rob died as he tried to set fire to Finn's bus on the eve of the new Millennium.

Lucy was both excited and terrified at the prospect of a life without Rob, and began to realize that her fear of him had been holding her back. After much soul-searching, Lucy decided that she wanted to travel the world and Tony offered to go with her. As Tony became increasingly preoccupied with researching tropical diseases, Lucy began to realize that he really didn't want to leave Hollyoaks and told him he should stay in Chester. As Lucy and Tony bid farewell at the airport, Tony promised Lucy that he'd wait for her, but Lucy left and we sensed that she would never return.

CHLOE BRUCE *played by Mikyla Dodd*

Chloe 'the moose' Bruce arrived on our screens back in March 2000. A school friend of Max's and O.B's, she soon proved her worth when she relieved them both of their virginity! They formed a close threesome, with the boys often enlisting Chloe to help them with money-making schemes – playing Mother Christmas when they started their own grotto! Chloe came into her own when she started at Hollyoaks Community College and became friends with the other students. She moved into Tony's house and after a one-night stand with Alex, soon found happiness with assistant caretaker Matt. For a time this relationship looked blissful, yet it went sour when Chloe began to have problems with her weight and self-perception and they split up. She is now trying to come to terms with her problems and attempting to find a Chloe she is comfortable being.

Name: Mikyla Dodd

Age: 24

Place of Birth: Blackburn

Earliest Memory: My dad tying a cushion to my bum so I wouldn't hurt myself roller-skating

Favourite Film: *Godfather* Parts I & II

Favourite Band: The Carpenters

Ideal Man: Darren Jeffries

Favourite holiday destination: New York

Who would you want to play you in a film of your life: Darren Jeffries

What three things would you take with you to a desert island: A Frank Sinatra CD, Dopey – my stuffed dwarf, and my fridge!

Tell me about your audition for *Hollyoaks*.

I came in and I had my hair all nicely blow-dried, looking all glam and then I realized it was for a seventeen-year-old! So I went to the toilets, washed my make-up off to reveal my teenage spots and put two little clips in the front of my hair and thought I *will* be seventeen! I then went in to the interview with Casting Director, Dorothy Andrew and Jo Hallows, Series Producer. From the moment I went in, I had a really good vibe off Jo. The only downside was when she asked me how old I was and I told her I was twenty-two! She looked shocked and I thought, 'No! It's all mine, it's in the bag and now it's been ripped away from me!' They asked me what I'd done before and I told them that I'd done this film about female sumo-wrestling and I thought Jo was going to fall off her chair from laughing! I said goodbye and before I got home there was a message on my answer-machine telling me that I'd got the job!

Your first episode was the late-night special featuring Luke's rape. What was it like appearing in such a prominent episode?

There was a lot of pressure because a lot of the cast at the time hadn't been directed by Jo [Hallows], so I got a bit jittery about that, but I thought that I'd rather be directed by someone I knew. I just thought that I could only do my best and after about the fourth or fifth take on the first day, Jo came up to me and said that I seemed insecure. I told her that I didn't know if I was doing it right; she said to me, 'Unless I say otherwise, you're doing a good job.' So that eased me into it. I remember we had a big cast viewing for the episode; normally you just slip in there in your episode and people miss your first three or four but Jimmy McKenna [Jack] came up to me afterwards and said, 'Well done, I hope they keep you here. I'm going to tell Jo and Phil I think you should stay!' so I thought I was well in there! It was nerve-wracking but it was in at the deep end, so anything after that was easy!

Chloe and Max shared their first sexual experience in the late-night episode. How was that?

Everybody has had a dodgy sexual experience and everybody said, 'I was just cringing' and that was how it was meant to be. It was a giggle to shoot, Matt [Max] and I were a bit nervous – for our first snog, we did a little kiss. Suddenly Jo said 'Cut!' and told us that we had to snog, she wanted the whole works!

What would you like to happen to Chloe?

One would like to get married! But then the worry is that you become boring as a married couple and no one wants to write for you! I think she should marry Matt, but then she should go off the rails, have an affair with Tony and split up with Matt. That should cover about eighty episodes! It would be a nice ending after they split up so tragically, and ultimately they do love each other.

CAROL GROVES, OCTOBER 2000

Played by Natalie Casey
January 1996–October 2000

Weird, wacky and one of the most unique and unconventional characters in the show, Carol Groves left Hollyoaks for a life on the open seas in October 2000.

Carol first appeared on our screens when she went on a double date with Lucy. A keen musician, who started The Crazy Bazz Studs with Lucy and Bazz, she had a life-changing moment when she was involved the crash that resulted in Dermot's death. Carol's near-death experience initiated her belief that she was psychic. Almost instantly, Carol allegedly had a gift for reading people's auras and an all-seeing eye, which helped her predict what was to come and alert her when there was trouble in the air. Undoubtedly Carol's spookiest moment was when she returned from Ireland and had a sinister premonition that something unwelcome was coming into their midst… Within moments, Lucy got a call telling her that Kurt had died.

Carol's kookiness continued throughout the rest of her time on the show and, whilst she had a brief attachment to Kurt, Carol seemed destined never to find a guy she genuinely liked, despite the odd dalliance with the likes of Tony in Newquay! That was until she met Finn and almost instantly fell head over heels in love. Of course, the path of true love never ran smoothly, and this tempestuous and often passionate relationship saw its fair share of ups and downs. Carol was also a loyal and trusted friend to Lucy, helping her get

First seen: On a double date with Lucy and Kurt at the bowling alley

Last seen: Boarding a cruise ship with her man in white

Finest moment: Returning the money Rob stole from Lucy back to the Bensons

Worst moment: When Rob tried to drown her in the bath

Funniest moment: As tour guide on Finn and Lewis's tour bus

Love of her life: Probably Finn, but the feelings were never reciprocated as strongly

Most embarrassing moment: Kissing Max and not remembering the next day

Most likely to say: 'I can see it in your aura…'

Least likely to say: 'No'. Carol got herself into no end of scrapes because of her inability to say no to any favour asked of her.

Place most likely to have been seen: Parkers, The Dog, her clairvoyant market stall

Hobbies/Interests: All things mystical, playing in the band

through the worst of her drug addiction. Her friendship with Lucy caused her to put her own life in jeopardy with Rob Hawthorne, but ultimately served to demonstrate just how dependable Carol was to those she loved.

After Lucy left, while she continued to get into scrapes with Tony and Finn, Carol missed having her best friend around. She soon turned her attentions to herself and became preoccupied with having a breast enlargement. Just before her operation, she read her tarot cards and discovered that she was destined to meet a man in a white suit. Assuming this was the doctor, she was dismayed to find him dressed in green and made a quick getaway!

Still feeling disillusioned, Carol agreed to help Finn and Lewis by singing at the opening night of The Loft. During her performance, she was spotted by a talent scout, who offered her a job singing on a cruise ship. After much soul-searching, Carol agreed to take the job. She arrived at the boat and was greeted by a uniformed officer – her man in white...

Carol returned briefly to *Hollyoaks* to appear in the Barcelona special, and heartstrings were pulled yet again as she and Tony realized that they had feelings for each other. Carol returned to her boat, but promised Tony that she would come back to him. Despite this promise, Carol never returned.

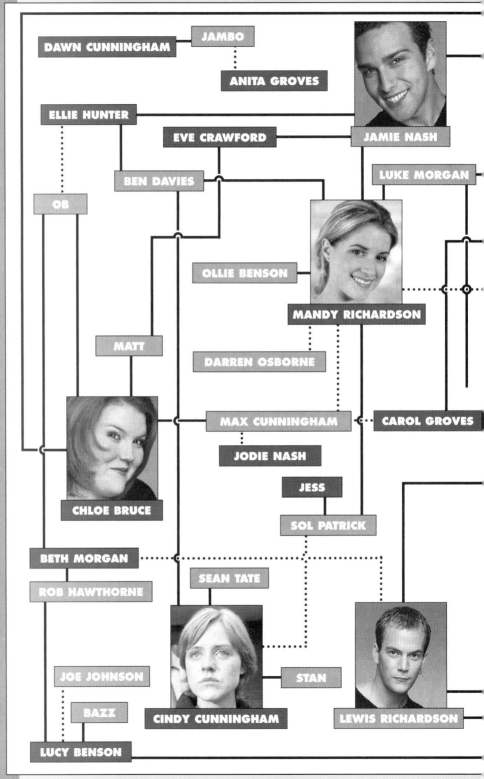

WHO SNOGGED WHO?

DAWN CUNNINGHAM — JAMBO
ANITA GROVES

ELLIE HUNTER
EVE CRAWFORD
JAMIE NASH

BEN DAVIES
LUKE MORGAN

OB

OLLIE BENSON
MANDY RICHARDSON

MATT
DARREN OSBORNE

MAX CUNNINGHAM — CAROL GROVES
JODIE NASH

CHLOE BRUCE
JESS

SOL PATRICK

BETH MORGAN
SEAN TATE

ROB HAWTHORNE

STAN

JOE JOHNSON

BAZZ
CINDY CUNNINGHAM
LEWIS RICHARDSON

LUCY BENSON

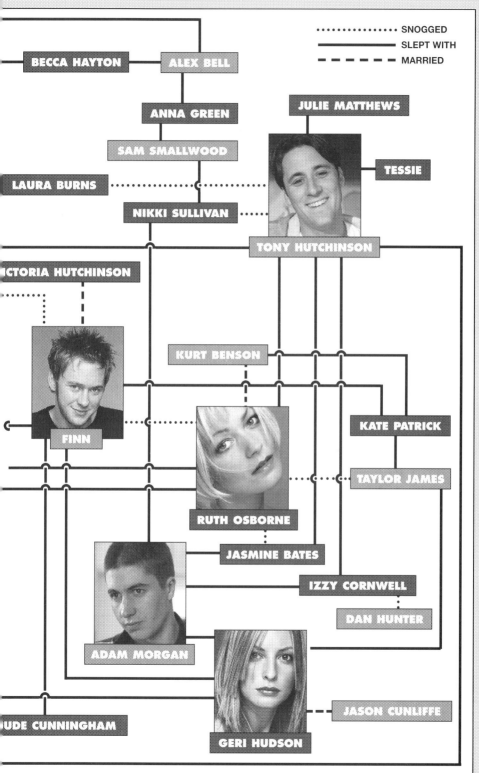

SNOGGED
SLEPT WITH
MARRIED

BECCA HAYTON

ALEX BELL

ANNA GREEN

JULIE MATTHEWS

SAM SMALLWOOD

TESSIE

LAURA BURNS

NIKKI SULLIVAN

TONY HUTCHINSON

CTORIA HUTCHINSON

KURT BENSON

FINN

KATE PATRICK

RUTH OSBORNE

TAYLOR JAMES

JASMINE BATES

IZZY CORNWELL

DAN HUNTER

ADAM MORGAN

UDE CUNNINGHAM

JASON CUNLIFFE

GERI HUDSON

BECCA HAYTON *played by Ali Bastian*

Becca Hayton first appeared on our screens in September 2001, when she arrived as a fresher at Hollyoaks Community College. She soon hooked up with Eve and, after moving into Tony's house, she fell for Jamie at exactly the same time that Eve had fallen for him. This ended in tears and she turned her attentions to Alex, but he soon lost interest when Anna gave birth to Charlie. A gossip, immature, yet sensitive, Becca has continued to be unlucky in love and seems fated never to meet a man who will treat her with any respect. Her major storyline to date was when she discovered that she had contracted gonorrhoea from Jamie. This compounded Becca's belief that the world was against her. Becca is destined to learn a few more life lessons before the end of her three-year course...

Name: Ali Bastian

Age: 20

Place of Birth: Windsor

Earliest Memory: Breaking my leg on a trampoline when I was three

Favourite Film: *Bridget Jones's Diary*

Favourite Band: Vacant Stare – friends of mine

Ideal Man: Athletic, tall, dark and handsome

Favourite holiday destination: The Maldives

Who would you want to play you in a film of your life: Gwyneth Paltrow

What three things would you take with you to a desert island: A good book, chocolate and a Walkman

What were you doing before you got the part in *Hollyoaks*?
I went to Redroofs Theatre School. I started there full-time when I was about ten and that's when I started working in the industry because they had an agency there. I did lots of bits and pieces; I played the young Jane Eyre in the BBC adaptation and then did some commercials. I left theatre school and went to do my A levels. After I completed them, I went back into the industry and was in a film called *Come Together* and then I got the part in *Hollyoaks*.

What do you think of Becca?
I think she's still got a lot of growing up to do; she can be a little bit immature. I think she's probably where I was about two years ago – she's in that place where relationships are the most important thing in her life.

Is Ali Bastian anything like Becca?
I like to think I don't whine as much! Becca's a bit of a victim, I hope she doesn't go on that way forever, I want her to toughen up a little bit.

What do you prefer, playing comedy or drama?

I prefer doing drama, I probably find that easier actually – stuff that requires high levels of focus. When you get some really well-written scripts and you totally get into it, I love doing that kind of work. Then again, recently, Becca's had this kind of clown element to her, she does some incredibly silly things, which is also fun to do.

Who else would you have liked to have played in *Hollyoaks*?

I would have liked to have had a go at playing a Geri-type character. It would have been fun, but then again, it's also nice to have a character who is as dippy and silly as Becca, it's nice to be able to let go and play with the character.

What advice would you give to aspiring actors out there?

To crack on, no matter what. There were times when I thought it wasn't going to happen and I got a lot of knock-backs. But if you want it enough and keep plodding on, it *will* happen – just never give up.

CINDY CUNNINGHAM, NOVEMBER 2000

Played by Stephanie Waring
November 1996–November 2000

Played by Laura Crossley
December 1995–November 1996

Of all the characters in *Hollyoaks*, Cindy Cunningham may well have had the roughest ride. Life was running pretty smoothly until the night of her sixteenth birthday when she succumbed to Stan's advances and unwittingly fell pregnant. Cindy concealed the pregnancy from her parents and, when she finally gave birth, abandoned her child and tried to carry on as normal.

Her parents reunited mother and child forcibly, but a desperate Cindy tried to suffocate baby Holly. The shock of this made her realize that she did in fact genuinely love her baby. Just as Cindy's life was finally going well again, she got together with the decorator Sean Tate, who proceeded to mistreat Holly, which came to a head when Holly burnt herself on a firework. This incident was brought to the attention of Social Services, who would continue to hound Cindy until she was forced to leave Chester in November 2000. A devastated Cindy was abandoned at the airport by Sean, losing all hope of a life abroad when Holly was prevented from leaving because she didn't have a passport. Instead, Cindy returned to Hollyoaks and tried once again to adapt to the role of single mother.

As Cindy settled into her new business venture, Steam Team, she met and

---

First seen: Going to Alton Towers with Natasha, Dawn and the girls

Last seen: At the airport with Holly, saying goodbye to Ben

Finest moment: Coping with her pregnancy without any help from her parents and giving up her family and friends for the sake of her child

Worst moment: Giving birth alone, abandoning her child and then finding out that her sister Dawn had died…

Funniest moment: Battling with Mandy over Ben Davies

Love of her life: She thought it was Sean but realized it wasn't, and she never had the chance to see if things would have worked out with Stan

Most embarrassing moment: When Mr Richardson discovered that she and Mandy had been collecting money for a non-existent donkey sanctuary!

Hobbies/Interests: Always wanted to study nursing, but having Holly prevented this

fell head over heels for Ben Davies, a trainee firefighter who had recently moved to the area. Still juggling work and motherhood, Cindy was working at The Loft and unable to find a babysitter, and so she had to take Holly to work with her. She left Holly sleeping in the club's cloakroom and, unbeknown to Cindy, Holly found an ecstasy tablet and swallowed it. As Holly was rushed to hospital, Cindy realized that it would only be a matter of time before Social Services would try to take Holly away from her.

A desperate Cindy concluded that she had no choice but to flee the country, as she couldn't bear to lose her child. She managed to persuade Ben to pick her up from the hospital and, as they made a mad dash to the airport, Cindy knocked Anna Green over. Desperate to get away, Cindy left Anna for dead, drove on to the airport and left with Holly. Ultimately, Cindy was a girl who was forced to grow up before her time, but the child she had resented more than anything was eventually the person for whom she gave up everything.

ZARA MORGAN *played by Kelly Greenwood*

Moody, impetuous, but highly intelligent, Zara was introduced as the youngest member of the Morgan clan back in April 1999. Zara struggled to settle into Chester and as a result caused endless trouble at her new school, culminating in her trying to burn down her school after an argument about her art project and she was sent for psychological assessment. Zara had been deeply affected by her parents' marriage problems and often found herself coming second to her elder siblings, especially Luke, who was trying to cope with his rape ordeal, and later Adam, after he was paralysed. Zara was friends with Steph, who proved to be a bad influence on her, and she later made friends with Abby, who proved to be a more grounded friend than Steph but who wasn't averse to getting into trouble. After causing trouble by inventing a fictitious relationship with Paul Millington, Zara set her sights on Brian, became a Goth and won his heart, only to later lose him to Steph and then to Lisa.

Name: Kelly Greenwood

Age: 19

Place of Birth: Salford

Earliest Memory: Being in a dancing competition with my little sister

Favourite Film: *Notting Hill*

Favourite Band: Toploader

Ideal Man: Robbie Williams

Favourite holiday destination: Mexico

Who would you want to play you in a film of your life: Thora Birch

What three things would you take with you to a desert island: My toothbrush, tweezers and chocolate

How did you get into acting?

I went to a drama agency and got an agent and started going to classes, and then went for a few auditions. My first audition was for *Children's Ward*. It was my first audition and I got the job! I was in eleven out of the twelve episodes and I was really nervous. I played a girl who was an asthmatic and spent nine of the episodes in hospital with asthma!

Can you remember your audition for *Hollyoaks*?

I think I was originally auditioning for Beth, because all the other girls seemed to be a lot older and then people were swapping around reading for Zara and then Beth. I just always read for Zara and then when I got the recall, I was reading for Zara and everyone else was reading for Beth.

How would you describe Zara?

Funny, weird and a bit temperamental. She's got a different side to her that she doesn't let a lot of people see.

Can you remember your first day on set?
I can remember that Eve (Mrs Morgan), Ross (Mr Morgan) and I had a meeting in Drive 'N' Buy with David Richardson, who was the Director at the time. It was a chat to stop us being nervous and make us feel more settled.

You've been in the show for over three years now; do you have a favourite episode?
I like all the stuff I did with the psychiatrist when I burnt the school down. I had to pretend to be remorseful that I'd done it and then you finally realized that it was just an act and Zara wasn't sorry that she did it. It was great leading everyone astray, believing that Zara was really sorry and was going to change although she never did.

What direction would you like to see Zara heading in?
When Zara first came into it, she was really clever and she was a bit of a swot and now I'm not sure if she's still clever... I'd like her to go to college and make friends with people and be nice, but she can't be too nice because that's boring.

WORKING IN TELEVISION

Fancy a career in television but don't know where to start or what you'd like to do? The following section is an opportunity for you to learn more about the workings of a television production company and, more importantly, the people behind the camera who bring *Hollyoaks* to your screens. The chart below should help you to understand the different departments involved in the production of *Hollyoaks*. If any of them interest you, flick to the Day in the Life section and find out what a typical day is like for them and what part they play in the production of the show. See what tips they have to offer on how to get into the industry, and learn more about the day-to-day challenges they face to get *Hollyoaks* onto the screen.

PRODUCERS

These are the decision-makers who guide the show from script to screen.

THE SCRIPT DEPARTMENT

Where the storylines are written and scripts are produced. The final scripts from this department are the catalyst for all other departments to begin work.

CASTING

If the scripts require any new characters, it is the job of Casting to find suitable actors and then organize auditions with the producers.

ADMINISTRATION

It is the job of Administration to organize the publication of all scripts, as well as making sure that all the relevant departments have copies of the scripts.

PRODUCTION

The production department organize the shoot of *Hollyoaks*. Their job includes organizing crews, scheduling actors and finding locations, as well as trying to squeeze the shoot of two episodes into six days.

WARDROBE

Wardrobe organize all costumes for the shoot. One wardrobe assistant will be assigned to a shoot of two episodes and will be in charge of all costumes in those particular episodes.

MAKE-UP

This department is responsible for 'making up' the actors every morning. A make-up artist will also be on set for the whole of the shoot to touch up the glamour as well as maintain the bruises!

DESIGN

Design prepare all of the sets and props for the shoot. This might involve anything from designing a gadget for Theo's shop or mocking up a fictitious newspaper, through to building a brand new set!

POST-PRODUCTION

This department starts work when the production on two episodes has finished. An editor will work with the director to cut the episode together and once the producers have viewed the two episodes, they will then go into Dub, where sound effects and music are added. Once this is completed, the episode is ready to go to Channel 4!

PUBLICITY

It is then down to Publicity to make sure that everybody knows about *Hollyoaks*!

Natasha Lund (Eve) discusses a scene with Director Chris Johnston.

A boom swinger records Sarah Dunn's (Mandy's) dialogue.

A DAY IN THE LIFE OF A SHOOT

Production is undoubtedly one of the most dynamic and versatile departments involved in the making of *Hollyoaks*. Production takes the finished script from the script department and, with its large crew, is responsible for organizing, planning and actually shooting the episode.

In the production crew, production managers assign crews to the directors and schedule all actors and scenes so that two episodes of *Hollyoaks* can be shot within six days. Working alongside the production managers are the location managers, who are responsible for finding locations for the shoots. For example, if a script depicted a scene where Zara and Abby go to the local fair, it would be the job of the locations department to find a nearby fair, ask for permission to film and then make sure that it was going to be available during the scheduled shoot. Also working in Production are production secretaries, who organize the call sheets, detailing all of the call times for artists and directors to be on the set, and all of the requirements for the day's shoot, including equipment and walk-ons (extras).

BEFORE THE SHOOT BEGINS

The first assistant director and production manager will first of all read the scripts and then break down the scenes into what they call shoot days. For example, all scenes to be shot in Drive 'N' Buy will be shot on day one, all scenes to be shot in The Dog will be shot on day two, etc. Also taken into consideration during scheduling are the scenes that take place in the day and scenes that take place at night. During this time, the second assistant director will arrange all the director's meetings with various departments, i.e. make-up, wardrobe and design, so that they can inform each department of their specific requirements for the shoot. For example, if the script had a scene with Mandy in The Loft, her costume and make-up would be very different from a day at college or waking up after a night out in The Loft. The director might also have

Jamie Luke (Norman) looks to see what scenes he is shooting that day.

specific prop requirements for the episode – for example, if a cup is going to be smashed, the design department will need to have at least six cups standing by.

The following week the director and the technical crew hold a recce and planning meeting. At this meeting, the location manager takes the crew and director to the location because each department has specific requirements on each location. The sparks (electricians) need power, the camera department need to work out positions for the cameras and the sound department need to check for excessive noise pollution. All departments need to know where to park their vehicles and most importantly, where the location caterers will be parked!

When the crew returns to headquarters, they hold a planning meeting where the schedule for the shoot is confirmed. The director will then discuss each scene individually, with the aid of his floor plans, so that each department knows what is planned for every day and what equipment is required, i.e. cameras, booms, radio mics, etc. The production assistant makes notes during this meeting to add all this additional information to the schedule. After the planning meeting, the co-ordinator issues the hours for each shoot day and books any additional staff required. They also allocate vehicles and equipment, and this is all added to the call sheet. The first assistant director then sits down with the director to discuss the time allocated for each scene on each day. Once this is completed, the crew is ready to begin shooting their two episodes.

A TYPICAL DAY...

The Scenario
The scene is set at 9.00am in Drive 'N' Buy. The scene is interior and features Mr C, Max, O.B. and Chloe.

The Crew
Director
First Assistant Director
Second Assistant Director (Assistant Floor Manager)
Production Assistant (Continuity)
Director of Photography
Camera Operator
Camera Assistant
Sound Mixer
Boom Operator and Second Boom Operator
Vision Engineer
Lighting Technician
Sparks (Electricians)
Wardrobe Assistant ⎫
Make-up Assistant ⎬ These will watch the shoot from the monitor
Studio Hand (design) ⎭ and record all continuity information.

Ali Bastian (Becca), Jamie Luke (Norman) and Lee Otway (Bombhead) check their lines before shooting a scene.

The four actors arrive on set at 8.00am. First of all, they have a block-through, where the director tells them where he'd like them to stand and what he'd like them to say in each particular position. Next, they have a line-run, where they walk through the scene with dialogue. The four actors then go in to Make-up and Wardrobe – the girls are allowed up to forty-five minutes to get ready and the boys only fifteen! Whilst the actors are in Make-up, the crew start rigging – putting up lights, setting down tracks and positioning the cameras. As soon as the actors are ready, the second assistant director (assistant floor manager) escorts them to the set and, when the floor is ready (i.e. everything is rigged), shooting commences on the first scene of the day.

Present on the set is the director, the first assistant director, the camera operator, the camera assistant and the boom operator. The first shot of the day is to be a wide shot of the Drive 'N' Buy scene, where you see all the action, requiring all four actors. Once the director is satisfied with the wide shot, mid-shots are taken, perhaps featuring just one actor and focussing on his/her reaction. After these, close shots are taken, focussing primarily on one character. A selection of shots may be taken at this point, to guarantee a close-up of each of the four characters, but the script will dictate which character the scene should focus on. For example, if the main feature of this Drive 'N' Buy scene is Chloe, then the director will focus many of the close shots on her.

Ideally, the crew needs to shoot about nine minutes of *Hollyoaks* a day. So, if an average scene runs for one and a half minutes, the crew would be trying to shoot six scenes a day. As the first scene of the day is in Drive 'N' Buy, the director will have scheduled the rest of the scenes for that day to be in the same location or in one close by, so that valuable time is not lost de-rigging and transporting equipment across to another location. So on this day, an ideal set of scenes would be two scenes in Drive 'N' Buy, a scene in the Village area and a scene in Finn's Yard as all the locations are close together.

Problems that occur on the shoot might include actors being double-booked for shoots and postponement due to an actor being ill. The weather can also have a major impact on a shoot – if the script dictates a sunny day and it's raining, either the script has to be amended to accommodate the rain, or the shoot has to be rescheduled for another day. In most instances, the scene will be shot in the weather conditions that prevail and the dialogue amended to accommodate it.

CAREERS

For anyone interested in a career in television production, there are several different ways to pursue one. Try contacting local production companies and asking for work experience as a runner, who does all the legwork on a shoot. This will provide you with an excellent insight into the workings of a crew, whilst also helping you to establish which particular side of production you are interested in. Once you have established this, one option is to try to get a permanent job as a runner, and see if there are opportunities within the television company for in-house training within a particular field of expertise. There are also colleges across the country offering media courses, many of which specialize in specific training in media production. Contact your local careers office for more detailed information.

For more information, check out the websites www.skillsformedia.com and www.skillset.org

A DAY IN THE LIFE OF WARDROBE

Alex McGregor and his wardrobe department have a hectic schedule. Not only do they have to make sure that the cast of *Hollyoaks* look desirable, they also have to choose clothes that tell us something about the characters wearing them. The department constantly has to reinvent the characters' wardrobes to remain one step ahead of ever-evolving fashion trends. The following is an insight into the frantic life of the *Hollyoaks* wardrobe department.

A TYPICAL DAY...

A typical morning would find Wardrobe out on the streets of Liverpool and Chester looking for clothes for the characters. They will have had a meeting the day before to discuss what clothes are needed, what looks they are intending to go for, and then in the morning will head out to hunt for suitable items. Often, they find themselves looking for one particular, and at times unusual, item of clothing that is required for a particular episode. Wardrobe then come into the office to sort out rosters and assign wardrobe assistants to specific shoots, as well as beginning to allocate costumes for specific characters. Alex also has to be on hand for meetings with producers about future storylines, as well as to make plans for the look of any new characters in the show. Wardrobe also has to check for any problems in Production, and then check that the wardrobe assistants have everything they need for the next day's shoot. In some instances, costumes will be made within Mersey Television, as some of the wardrobe team are trained in fashion design.

WHERE WARDROBE SHOP FOR THE GIRLS

The majority of the girls' clothes come from TopShop, although Wardrobe often finds outfits in shops such as Oasis, Warehouse, Zara, Kookaï and Hennes.

Alex McGregor showing Lisa Kay (Anna) her wardrobe.

The majority of the boys' wardrobe comes from Topman, where they have an extensive line of Levi jeans. They get most of the boys' T-shirts from Topman, Gap or French Connection.

Costumes will generally be made in-house for special episodes, such as the Golden Jubilee extravaganza, where Wardrobe had to provide costumes for the main characters – who in this instance were all dressed as Kings and Queens of England – as well as providing costumes for the extras.

Wardrobe assistants are required to follow a block of episodes, and often spend long hours on set, logging costume requirements and taking continuity photos. It is the wardrobe assistant's job to guarantee that the continuity of a costume is maintained – tiny details, such as whether or not a button is undone, all have to be recorded so that if they ever have to re-shoot a scene, there will be no change in the appearance of the characters' clothes. Producers will occasionally demand a re-shoot of a scene as much as a month after it had originally been shot. It is then down to Wardrobe and Make-up to guarantee that the character looks exactly the same as they did a month ago. The wardrobe assistants are also responsible for all the washing and ironing of costumes, making sure that they look perfect. In some instances, such as a food fight, Wardrobe has to buy three or four replicas of the same items of clothing, so that they are on hand to provide clean replacements if the director wants to shoot the scene again.

Every character has an assigned wardrobe that is just for their character. You will never see Dan wearing anything from Ben's wardrobe, for example, as each character has an individual look that has been carefully planned. All of the costumes are kept on rails assigned to each character and the wardrobe assistants use this to decide what outfit the character will be wearing. Like Make-up, Wardrobe decides what a character will wear by assessing the character profiles, and, as most of the characters are students, Wardrobe tend to find outfits that look good, but aren't necessarily expensive.

A typical day in Wardrobe is never destined to run smoothly and there have been several occasions when Wardrobe have had to overcome mini disasters. Clothes can go missing, resulting in Wardrobe having a mad dash to try to find a replacement. If the team can't find the same item again, they often have to improvise and make alterations to a similar-looking outfit. Occasionally, wardrobe will be surprised by a sudden requirement for an unusual costume and will have to make an unexpected trip to the shops to find something suitable.

CAREERS

For any readers interested in a career in Wardrobe, there are several different routes into the industry. There are some opportunities for in-house training with television companies. Alternatively, there are several universities offering degrees in fashion, textile design, as well as establishments dedicated primarily to fashion, such as The London College of Fashion. For more information, check out the websites www.skillsformedia.com and www.skillset.org

A DAY IN THE LIFE OF MAKE-UP

The show stars some of the most beautiful girls on television and yet Helen Black and her team of make-up artists still have no easy task in ensuring that the girls continue to remain the objects of affection for millions of male viewers across the country.

Not only does the make-up department have to keep the girls looking beautiful, it also has to be prepared to inflict bruises, sudden ageing and spots at the drop of a hat! Read on to learn about a typical day in the life of a department that plays an integral part in the show's success.

> ### GENERAL MAKE-UP USED ON THE GIRLS
>
> - Max Factor bases in soft beige tones
> - Christian Dior eyeshadows
> - At Christmas, the girls tend to use Boots No 17, Limited Edition (which is usually bright, glittery colours!)

A TYPICAL DAY...

A typical day starts at 8.00am and finishes at around 19.00 in the evening, or often later. If an actor is needed on set by 8.30am, depending on who it is and what make-up is required, they will be called half an hour before they are due on set. As well as having make-up applied during this time, the artist has to get into costume. If the scene to be filmed is a morning scene, where a female character has just got up, the make-up artist will first of all apply a foundation or concealer, then a light application of brown or clear mascara and possibly a little lip balm. This light application gives the impression that the actor is wearing little or no make-up when they first wake up. The make-up team won't dress the hair until the actor comes back from wardrobe in costume. If the make-up team are preparing the girls for a day scene, then they will still only apply light make-up, depending on the character. Make-up is also used to reflect character in the show, so Ellie Hunter's make-up, for example, someone who is concerned about her appearance, would be more defined, to make it clear to the audience that she has taken the time to look good. There are several instances where the girls find themselves spending a lot longer in Make-up. For Geri's wedding, Joanna Taylor (Geri) and Sarah Jayne Steed (Alyson) were in Make-up for almost two hours. Far more time was taken on their hair and make-up on this occasion because the wedding was such an elaborate affair and Geri had to look stunning. To deal with special episodes like this, requiring such meticulous work, the make-up department tends to bring extra people in to help.

Once the actor is finished in Make-up, the make-up artist overseeing the shoot will be responsible for maintaining the specific look required by the director for their block of episodes. The make-up artist is responsible for ensuring that their assistant in the make-up department also knows what look is required for the character. The assigned make-up artist spends most of the day on set, providing assistance to the girls, who will need their make-up touched up. There are constant checks to make sure that there is complete continuity in the hair and the make-up of a character. Often a scene – for example, one with Mandy in The Loft – might be split and shot over two consecutive weeks. The make-up artist needs to make sure that Mandy looks exactly the same as she did in the scene shot the previous week. To achieve this, the make-up artist is responsible for logging all the information about the character's make-up and hair. They do this by taking Polaroids of the actors, known as continuity photographs, which they can refer to when filming the rest of the scenes in that block of episodes.

Make-up decides on the look of a character through consultation with the producers. The producers explain how they perceive a character and the make-up department try to convey these traits. For example, a stressed-out mother of three would have no time to apply much make-up and so the make-up department would use only a light application to convey this. Students might spend more money on make-up and so the make-up department tend to use more expensive products on the likes of Becca and Izzy, showing that these girls dedicate more care and time to their appearance. With the younger characters, the make-up department tends to look at what is popular in the public arena – TV shows, pop stars, and emulate the current look.

The make-up department faces constant challenges, most often when characters become ill and make-up is needed to depict this. Undoubtedly, the most challenging look to achieve was that of the dying Lewis Richardson. Because Lewis's death was featured in *Hollyoaks: Movin' On*, which was broadcast late at night, the make-up department had more scope to depict his condition with a higher level of realism. Lewis was suffering from jaundice caused by liver failure, so they had to make him look yellow, albeit as realistically and as shockingly as possible. Jaundice victims often have yellow eyes, and so the team tried various methods to make actor Ben Hull's eyes look

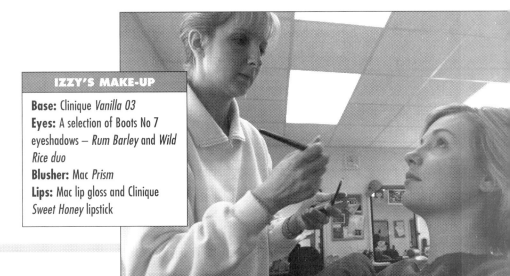

IZZY'S MAKE-UP

Base: Clinique *Vanilla 03*
Eyes: A selection of Boots No 7 eyeshadows – *Rum Barley* and *Wild Rice* duo
Blusher: Mac *Prism*
Lips: Mac lip gloss and Clinique *Sweet Honey* lipstick

yellow. They tried yellow eye drops, but when these failed to have the desired effect, they struck upon the idea of using yellow contact lenses. The department also faced the challenge of providing make-up for Ruth after Lewis had attacked her. Ruth had suffered extensive facial injuries, and so the make-up department made a cast for Terri Dwyer's face to accentuate the swelling of her eyes and bruising on her face.

The male members of the cast tend to spend less time in Make-up. Make-up generally checks that the boys are clean-shaven, and then applies a light, translucent base that can't be detected on camera and a touch of powder to stop their faces from shining.

If actors want to change their image, meticulous planning has to take place between the producers and the make-up department so that continuity on screen will not be affected. At times, Make-up have had their work cut out trying to cover up for a change in image, and there have been several instances where an actor has had their hair cut and then been called in for re-shoots. In some desperate situations, make-up has had to apply hair extensions in an attempt to achieve perfect continuity!

CAREERS

If any readers are interested in a career in Make-up, then there are two paths they could pursue. The first is in-house training within a production company, where training takes place on the job. The second is a film and television make-up course. Some of these courses are self-funded, but they do offer thorough training in the art of make-up for television and film. Two such establishments are Greasepaint (Telephone 020 8840 6000) and the London College of Fashion (020 7514 7400). Make-up departments also advise trying to get some work experience – make enquiries to your local council as to whether it has a film office. You could contact them and volunteer your services to their make-up department. Film sets often need help applying make-up to extras, which can often run into hundreds!

For more information, check out the websites **www.skillsformedia.com** and **www.skillset.org**

MANDY'S MAKE-UP

Base: Clinique *Vanilla 03*
Eyes: A selection of Mac eyeshadows – *Jest* and *Shale*
Blusher: Mac *Prism*
Lips: Mac lust lip gloss – *Oh baby* and *Prrr...*

A DAY IN THE LIFE OF PUBLICITY

It is Publicity's job to maintain public awareness about *Hollyoaks* by securing press coverage for the show; what follows is a typical day.

A TYPICAL DAY...

First, they check the newspapers and cut out anything that has been written about the show. The next job is to respond to any emails that have been sent, possibly from news agencies commenting on reports in the papers, or from radio and television programmes or magazines wanting to arrange interviews and photo shoots with the cast members. For example, if a magazine wanted to do a feature on the *Hollyoaks* girls, Publicity will find out what the article will be about, and where and when photos will be shot. These shoots need to be planned meticulously with Production to ensure that the filming of the show is not affected. Susan Wilks and Gemma Hayden (the publicists) will chaperone the actors on these occasions, monitoring the shoot, and checking that actors don't reveal too much about future storylines. Publicity will often ask to approve interviews and photo shoots prior to publication, to make sure that the actor hasn't been misquoted, and that photos are not published that the actor might not be happy with. After emails have been dealt with, calls from magazines and newspapers start to come in, many of them asking for synopses of the show, or for future storylines to include in TV listings. A magazine doing a feature on Beth Morgan's court case, for example, would request a telephone interview with the actress who plays Beth. Publicity would also provide some background to the story, as well as photographs of the episode to include in the publication. Teen magazines often call up to do quick profiles of actors over the phone. Publicity also receives numerous requests from charities asking for actors to help launch schemes – using characters from a show like *Hollyoaks* can be a great endorsement.

In addition to responding to enquiries, the publicity office proactively contacts the press to run features on particular issues. Often when *Hollyoaks* is about to broadcast a particularly controversial storyline, such as Lewis's suicide, the media will want a spokesperson to comment on the story. Publicity also organize launches for particular milestones of the show. When *Hollyoaks* went from three nights a week to four, Publicity organized a launch in London, and invited all the leading newspapers and magazines in an attempt to maximize exposure.

CAREERS

The most common way into PR is to study PR or communications at either degree or diploma level, although some companies offer in-house training. A good way of getting ahead is to contact a local organization for work experience – even doing some PR for your local rugby club will look good on your CV. To find out more, check out www.skillsformedia.com and www.skillset.org

A DAY IN THE LIFE OF A PRODUCER

A producer is the decision-maker who guides the show from script to screen from the initial stage in the storyline meeting, through to its arrival on our screens. One of the most time-consuming parts of being a producer on *Hollyoaks* is working on the scripts – each one has at least three drafts, sometimes more. It is down to the producers to steer the scripts through each draft, so that the writers achieve the very best results. As well as working on the scripts, the producers have to maintain a general overview of the programme and be constantly thinking up ideas that might move the show forward. As the market for soaps continues to expand, *Hollyoaks* needs to stay one step ahead of its competition. It is the producer's job to ensure that *Hollyoaks* achieves this goal...

The following interview is a brief glimpse into a typical day's work of a producer on *Hollyoaks*. Working alongside Executive Producer Phil Redmond, Jo Hallows has been leading the *Hollyoaks* team since December 1995. Not only has she had to guide *Hollyoaks* from a once-weekly show to its current four times a week status, Jo has also directed some of the show's acclaimed episodes, beginning with the death of Natasha through to Luke's rape.

What's a typical day for you on *Hollyoaks*?
The main job is to plan the future of the show. You constantly have to look ahead, deciding *what* you want, *how* to shape the programme and *how* to bring in new characters and ideas. There are always stories that resurface and it's down to the producer to find the best possible time for the storylines to be incorporated into the show. Another major part of the job is driving the team forwards and maintaining motivation. Whilst the writers come up with a lot of the ideas, it is a matter of taking the best ones and moulding them so that we use them at just the right time. The male rape story was the classic example – the story idea came up three times, but I hadn't come up with the right scenario for it. It was on the third instance that we finally realized that it would be the perfect story for Luke.

What storylines do you think *Hollyoaks* should be most proud of?
Certainly the Ruth and Lewis story. That was a very real situation and in hindsight I think we did it well. It had always been our intention to accentuate the horror of suicide and to convey the message that people regret taking such drastic action. We always strive to tackle difficult subjects, for example the recent Sexually Transmitted Infection storyline with Becca and Jamie. This is currently dominant in the news and because of this, it is this story that is hitting home with the audience.

For you, who have been the most memorable characters in the show?
I really liked Jude, because she was a ballsy character. Most people enjoyed writing for her and the audience loved her because she *always* did what you

dreamt about doing. Luke was another great character, he was very vulnerable and you couldn't help but love him. I liked Jambo; he was a real lateral thinker and was a fun character to work with. Tony is another fantastic character and after seven years, Nick Pickard has made it his own. Tony's easy to write for, because you can throw any story at him, both serious and frivolous, and you know that Nick will make a good job of it. He'll make you laugh and he'll also make you cry. He's probably the person I've cried at the most, some of the more difficult stories he's done, even though you know the story that's coming up, you can't help but have a lump in your throat…

What would you recommend to someone interested in a career in producing?
You've got to have determination and stamina! You've also got to have a *lot* of ideas and be able to drive people through them, because *Hollyoaks* at four nights a week is relentless. You have to know how to deal with a big team of people and manage them. The main attribute is that you have to have lots of ideas; soaps eat up ideas and it is down to the producer to make sure that *Hollyoaks* remains exciting and innovative.

Jo Hallows

DAN HUNTER *played by Andrew McNair*

Dan arrived in the show in style in April 2001, when he immediately caused a stir at Hollyoaks Community College by rebelling against the college car-parking system! From the start it was obvious that the Hunters had their fair share of problems. These became more apparent as we learned about Lisa's self-harming and Ellie's disappearance in Ibiza, and we learnt that Dan was a diabetic. Dan had taken all of these problems on his shoulders and he was the archetypal 'angry young man'. He has led quite a solitary existence since he arrived in the show, although he has found friendship with Ben Davies. Despite tempting offers from both Geri and Izzy, Dan's first priority remains his family and the garage. His only relief from these problems are his burnouts and his rally-racing. Dan assumed his problems would be over when Ellie returned home. Little did he know they were just beginning…

Name: Andrew McNair

Age: 22

Place of Birth: Salford

Earliest Memory: Wearing my dad's football boots trying to kick a ball

Favourite Film: *Goodfellas*

Favourite Band: Bruce Springsteen and the E-Street Band

Ideal Woman: Tall, beautiful, smart, intelligent, sexy — basically my fiancée, Rebecca

Favourite holiday destination: Marbella

Who would you want to play you in a film of your life: Me (why turn the work down?)

What three things would you take with you to a desert island: Rebecca, mini DVD player and DVD's, and my fishing tackle

How did you get into acting?

I was modelling down in London and started to move into TV presenting. I did a bit of stuff for *The Clothes Show* and *Pop 2000*. One day my agent phoned up and asked if I'd be interested in going to the *Hollyoaks* auditions. I said, 'Yes' immediately, and went there not knowing what to expect. I'd not really done anything beforehand — I'd done a few acting workshops, but nothing major. I went for the audition, got a recall two weeks later and had to audition again, this time with actors auditioning for Les and actresses auditioning for Lisa. I got a phone call twenty minutes after arriving home, telling me that I'd got the part. I was amazed; I jumped up and smacked my head on the door frame!

Is there much of Andy in Dan?

None at all! That's why it's so enjoyable for me to play him, because he's such a prat. He's miserable, a male chauvinist and is constantly angry with everybody. I get to come in every day and whinge.

Do you think Dan needs a girlfriend?
I don't think Dan will ever have one!
What he needs first and foremost are
mates – proper mates that he actually
gets on with. At the moment anyone
that says 'Hello' to him, he just whinges
at! He gets on very well with Ben,
although he doesn't see much of him.
They both understand each other's
area of life that they don't want to talk
about.

**Do you find it difficult shaking off
Dan when you go home?**
I'm a right grump when I go home! If
you're doing ten hours a day, seven
days a week, you can't switch off.
Sometimes you say things and then you
think, 'That's not me!' I like living away
so I have a nice drive home and I get to
switch off and forget about work!

What storyline have you most enjoyed?
The rally-driving without a shadow of a doubt. I had never done anything like
that before. I had a rally lesson before the episode with a rally-driver. When I
got out of the car, my body was aching from holding onto the car and laughing. I just couldn't stop laughing as I was going round the track.

Is there anyone else you would have liked to have played in the show?
Luke had a great character and had some really good storylines. I also like
Tony's character because he's just a pain; he's a complete fool. You imagine
him to be like one of those next-door neighbours who won't give kids their
ball back. He's one of those characters that all soaps need – a meddler, he's
a young Mr C.

Dan's had Izzy and Geri chasing him – what went wrong?
They just catch him at the wrong time, which is basically every time. There's
never a right time for Dan; the last thing on his mind is women. He's got too
much on his plate for things like that. The women in his life have had a major
impact on him – his sister was missing for two years; his mum was constantly
flying abroad and his younger sister is cutting herself. I think Dan's got this
underlying issue where he really doesn't trust women!

SOL PATRICK, APRIL 2001

Played by Paul Danan
November 1997 to April 2001

Mean, moody and volatile, to the outsider Sol was just a troublemaker who wasn't worth bothering with; but to those who knew him, Sol was a misunderstood and sensitive guy, whose unconventional upbringing and determination to protect his family were among his most redeeming features. Sol arrived on our screens back in November 1997, when he was introduced as the wayward son of Jill Patrick (Lynda Rooke), Jack Osborne's new barmaid.

He had a penchant for stealing cars whenever he felt frustrated and tended to burn off energy through joyriding. He began to change his ways when he met and fell for Mandy Richardson, but when she disappeared Sol found himself under suspicion. He was devastated when Mandy returned and called it all off. Sol returned to his old tricks, but life took another downward spiral when his older sister Kate began a search for her father, and Sol and his younger sister, Gina, discovered through Ruth that Jill was not their real mother. A distraught Jill told Gina and Sol the story of their mother's suicide and how she brought them up as her own, but they both reacted badly to the news and left home. The family was reunited, however, when Jill was seriously injured in her car, which Sol had taken without permission. Jill's accident shocked Sol into realizing quite how much she meant to him.

Just as Sol was beginning to get his life on track, he was shocked to be sentenced to twenty-eight days' imprisonment for driving without a licence. This was a harrowing experience for him, especially when he woke one morning to discover his cellmate had hanged himself. Sol was released from prison

DID YOU KNOW...?

Some of the writers needed a family tree for the Patrick family to follow the story of how they are all related!

First seen: Grabbing Mr Richardson in The Dog for being rude about his mother

Last seen: Boarding a bus with Jess, hoping to make a new life for himself in Spain

Finest moment: Saving prostitute Jess from a life on the streets

Worst moment: When Jill died from a brain tumour

Funniest moment: When he had to kiss a line-up of old women after Finn discovered that he'd stolen his Santa suit!

Love of his life: Jess — he risked his own life to save her from the clutches of her pimp, Steve

Most embarrassing moment: Being soaked by Darren when they fell out about the car-washing business

Most likely to say: 'It wasn't me' — Sol had an almost comical habit of getting himself into trouble

Least likely to say: 'Whatever you say...' — Sol refused to accept advice from anyone and insisted on living life by his own rules

Place most likely to have been seen: Usually in The Dog, though the volatile Sol would often fall out with Jack and Jill, and end up sleeping rough

Hobbies/Interests: Making money — he had dreams of a car-washing empire that, unsurprisingly, failed miserably

a changed man and settled back into life again by starting a car-washing business. However, his happiness was short-lived when he found out that Jill had a fatal brain tumour. He was devastated when she eventually lost her battle against the disease.

Sol struggled to come to terms with Jill's death and soon found himself back in trouble when he hooked up with teenage prostitute, Jess (Frankie Hough), a girl he had met whilst living on the streets. Sol soon became devoted to Jess's cause and his attempts at trying to rescue her from her pimp, Steve, provoked Steve into taking revenge by setting fire to The Dog. Sol carried on regardless, intent on building a new life with Jess and even after Steve kidnapped his sister, Gina, Sol still refused to let Jess return to the streets. Things got even nastier when Steve tried to take Jess back by force and, in a desperate struggle, Jess inadvertently pushed him over the fire escape of The Loft, almost killing him in the process. It was only a matter of time before the police would arrest Jess, and so Sol made the difficult decision to leave Chester and build a new life for them both in Ibiza. He bid a sad farewell to his surrogate father, Jack, and headed for the bus station. The police were by now in pursuit of Jess, but when Will Davies saw them boarding the bus, he decided to let them go, knowing that Jess deserved this second chance of happiness.

ELLIE HUNTER *played by Sarah Baxendale*

Ellie Hunter exploded onto our screens in February 2002, when she arrived back in Chester after a two-year absence, when she'd quite simply gone on holiday to Ibiza and never come back. Independent, gregarious and ultimately selfish, Ellie arrived home oblivious to the trauma she had caused her family over the past two years. After two years of looking after herself she is determined not to be pressurized by her family into doing anything she doesn't want to. She is out to have fun and will let nothing and no one stand in her way. Ellie reveals her more sensitive side when it comes to looking after Lee and Lisa, for whom she shows genuine affection. She brought them up whilst her mother went back to university and will do anything to protect them. This is in stark contrast to her relationship with Dan, which is very much one of love and hate.

Name: Sarah Baxendale

Age: 23

Place of Birth: Salford

Earliest Memory: My parents collecting me from school — they told me I was going to have a brother or sister! I was over the moon

Favourite Film: *Bridget Jones's Diary*

Favourite Band: Oasis

Ideal Man: Damon Albarn

Favourite holiday destination: The Maldives

Who would you want to play you in a film of your life: Jane Horrocks

What three things would you take with you to a desert island: A phone, suntan cream and water!

How did you get into acting?

I started acting at college and school, and got interested in it quite early. I did my A levels, auditioned for Rose Bruford drama school and got in. I was there for three years and really enjoyed it. I did my showcase, got a London agent and my first job was doing a theatre tour. I then had parts in *Fat Friends, My Beautiful Son* and *Doctors* and then landed the part of Ellie!

What was your audition for *Hollyoaks* like?

There were quite a few of us and it was like a sea of blondes when I walked in! So I went in for my audition and didn't know how I'd done, because it was just so quick. I then got a recall and after another audition it was down to just three of us. I then had to come back and there was another set of girls and only me out of the other three. That was the most nervous I've ever felt in an audition because it was *so* close. I went in for a *fifth* time — by that point I was starting to get really shaky but managed to control it. I knew I was doing something right because I'd been in five times. It was a mixture of feelings — excitement and complete disbelief that I could possibly be sat there. I then got a phone call telling me that I would start work in January!

Were you a fan of the show before you auditioned?

Yes! That made it all the more nerve-wracking on my first day because I knew I was going to recognize people and know they're not going to be like their characters.

Was it daunting to know the character of Ellie had been talked about so much before you arrived? Did you worry that the audience had already built up a picture of her?

You want to live up to people's expectations, but it's been good to have had the character already developed and it's been fun trying to bring that character alive. It's been great to have a ready-made family before I arrived – it meant that I got to know people really quickly and through working with the same people over and over again, you become quite close to them. I also love the fact that we all have similar accents! And some of us actually look like each other.

How would you describe Ellie?

I'd say she is selfish without trying to be. She's had two years of not having to think about anybody else but herself and enjoying herself. She's quite

outrageous; she craves fun, taking risks and excitement. She's got love in her – she's caring, especially towards Lisa, but she's also very defensive because of deep-rooted problems in the family.

Is Sarah anything like Ellie?

To a point, but she's much more extreme than me – everybody wants to go out and have a good time, but she pushes it to the limit. I always think about how people are and want to make people happy all the time. I'm very rarely rude to people or shout at them, but because I'm not like that, it's even more to fun to play! You can get anything that's inside you out on screen but you're forgiven for it because you're acting!

LUKE MORGAN, DECEMBER 2001

Played by Gary Lucy
March 1999–December 2001

If ever there was a character that the audience of *Hollyoaks* has nurtured and taken under its wing, it was Luke. After arriving as the charming and cocky sixteen year old who managed to seduce both the beautiful Ruth Osborne and the lovely Mandy Richardson, Luke was forced to grow up overnight when he was the victim of a shocking sex attack. Never has an audience reacted so strongly to a storyline and because of this, Luke built up a rapport with the audience unrivalled by any other character. His despair as he agonized over whether to tell his parents and later the police was felt by millions. The audience was desperate for Luke to recover from his ordeal, and felt as victorious as he did when Mark Gibbs was finally found guilty.

First seen: Chatting up an unsuspecting Ruth Osborne at Hollyoaks Community College

Last seen: In a taxi heading towards the airport on his way to Canada

Finest moment: When Mark Gibbs was found guilty of rape

Worst moment: The horrific night he was raped by Mark

Funniest moment: Being dumped by Ruth when she found out he was only sixteen!

Love of his life: Mandy Richardson, from the moment he saw her poster on the side of Finn's bus

Most embarrassing moment: Modelling thermal underwear and then finding out the pictures would be published in the local paper!

Most likely to say: Something charming – Luke was the ultimate ladies' man, managing to seduce both Mandy and Ruth

Least likely to say: 'I'll do an extra shift' – Deva was the bane of Luke's life and he much preferred playing football to helping out with his parents' business!

Place most likely to have been seen: Deva – working, The Dog and The Loft – at play!

Hobbies/Interests: Football and cars. Luke's love of football was the reason he left for Canada.

As Luke struggled to piece his life back together, he was once again an unwitting victim when he found out that Mandy had started dating his close friend, Ben Davies. Once again, the audience were on his side, anxious for him to find some sort of happiness and angry at Mandy for hurting him. Luke had a brief dalliance with the peculiar Laura and, after that fizzled out, Luke and Mandy both realized that they were right for one another after all. However, their relationship was tragically cut short when Mandy's brother Lewis committed suicide – suddenly Mandy was in no fit state to be pursuing a relationship, and Luke was once again left on his own.

It was because of this, in addition to the fact that Chester carried so many bad memories for him, that Luke decided to make some constructive changes to his life. He started football training with young kids and, as he began to enjoy this, he decided to make a clean break and pursue a job at a football training camp in Canada. Luke bid a sad farewell to Hollyoaks, pleased to be leaving memories of Mark Gibbs behind him, but sad to say goodbye to his family, especially Adam, who had been a rock of support for him after his rape ordeal. Sadly, Mandy never got to say goodbye to Luke, arriving on the scene just as his cab drove away; so the audience will have to wait and see whether *Hollyoaks*'s most popular couple will ever be reunited...

LISA HUNTER *played by Gemma Atkinson*

Shy, sensitive and introverted, Lisa Hunter arrived at Hollyoaks Comprehensive in April 2001. Unlike her older brother, Lee, Lisa had taken the brunt of her family's issues on her shoulders and took every family argument to heart. Lisa found it difficult fitting in at school and her shy and reserved manner soon became a morbid fascination for Zara, Abby and Steph. They knew that Lisa had a secret and it was finally revealed to the audience in November 2001, that Lisa self-harmed. In desperation at her family's troubles, she turned their problems onto herself – this was her way of coping. She was devastated when Lee, and then later her family, found out her secret. Their inability to cope with her self-harm only made it worse.

Name: Gemma Atkinson

Age: 17

Place of Birth: Bury

Earliest Memory: Learning to ride my bike

Favourite Film: *Scarface*

Favourite Band: Destiny's Child

Ideal Man: Josh Hartnett

Favourite holiday destination: Majorca

Who would you want to play you in a film of your life: Julia Roberts

What three things would you take with you to a desert island: A CD player, a box of Celebrations and suncream

She found solace and comfort in the arms of Brian, provoking the wrath of Zara in the process. Brian helped Lisa to find another way of externalizing her emotions – by singing and writing songs. Lisa was devastated by Ellie's disappearance and was overjoyed when she finally returned after two years; at last, there was someone in her family who understood her.

How did you get into acting?
I joined Manchester Model Agency when I was about fifteen. I did modelling for about nine or ten months and then got a casting for *Hollyoaks,* came along and got it!

Can you remember your audition?
Yeah, I was quite nervous. There were about twelve girls and twelve lads all in the one little room that was boiling hot. They called us in one at a time and we did a read-through in front of the camera and then they narrowed it down to just me and this other girl. We had to wait about five hours and then we did a read-through with Les and Dan, and then they rang me when I got home and told me that I'd got the part.

What was your first day on set like?
It was on location at the school with Kelly [Zara], Jonathan [Brian] and Helen [Abby]. I enjoyed it, but it was a little weird as there were a lot of things I didn't understand as we were shooting – 'play it like this' and 'like that'. I'd not done any acting before so it was all a bit confusing but Jonathan told me what it all meant.

How did you feel when you found out about Lisa's self-harm storyline?
I saw it as a real chance to prove myself as an actress. The response from the viewers about the storyline has been really positive, which has shown that we're doing it right. It's a bit upsetting to read the scripts and know that people really are cutting themselves. The self-harm story is going to continue for quite some time – Lisa's going to get worse before she starts to get any better…

What's been your favourite episode?
Probably the New Year's Eve episode when I started seeing Brian. It was the first kissing scene that I did, and because the viewers had wanted Lisa and Brian to get together for so long, when we finally filmed it Jonathan and I wanted to try and make the kissing scene the best scene that we'd ever done.

What would you like to happen to Lisa?
Hopefully she'll go to college and get a new set of friends, where she's the popular one and isn't being bullied. Hopefully, she won't start trying to get her own back by bullying other people, she'll just have a good set of friends and enjoy college life.

Is Gemma anything like Lisa?
No, if someone was bullying me, I'd do something about it! I also wouldn't go out with a lad who wore make-up!

GERI HUDSON, DECEMBER 2001

Played by Joanna Taylor
September 1999–December 2001

Without doubt one of the most gutsy and larger-than-life characters in the show, Geri Hudson left *Hollyoaks* with indelible memories when she said goodbye. She arrived as a fresher at Hollyoaks Community College in September 1999, and within months had become one of the most desired and popular characters in the show.

With the possible exception of Jude, there has yet to be another female character to rival the massive popularity of Geri. Admired by female viewers for her gutsiness and sharp wit, and lusted after by male viewers for her beauty, millions of viewers were sad to bid farewell to Geri when she left Chester for a life in Spain.

Geri was the rich daughter of a biscuit factory owner and academia was never high on her list of priorities. She arrived in Chester determined to have as much fun as she possibly could. Geri moved into halls with Sam, Nikki, Anna and Alex, and soon formed a strong friendship with Anna that would last throughout her time in Chester. Geri hooked up with Finn, but was dropped by him when he returned to Carol. After much teasing, she finally got together with Adam Morgan. However, this relationship was also scuppered when Adam lost interest in her over new fresher Izzy. Spurned by Adam, Geri

First seen: Arriving in her sports car, and asking Adam for directions to Hollyoaks Halls of Residence

Last seen: In her wedding dress, driving off in a limousine with her mother, Jacqui

Finest moment: Beating Izzy in the final round of Game 4 IT!

Worst moment: Discovering the 'real' Jason Cunliffe when he failed to protect her from Scott

Funniest moment: The Bottycelli Booth! Geri's film project where she filmed people's bottoms!

Love of her life: Certainly not Jason, possibly Adam Morgan, but neither have realized it yet

Most embarrassing moment: Being arrested for begging when dressed as an old woman after she was an extra in a film

Most likely to say: 'Work can wait until tomorrow' — Geri was never the most diligent of students, preferring the social aspect of college life!

Least likely to say: 'Apology accepted' — Geri revelled in her catfights, especially with Nikki and Izzy, her two sworn enemies

Place most likely to have been seen: The Dog and The Loft — Geri was a keen socialite and was never one to miss out on a drinking session

Hobbies/Interests: Being pampered and idolized — Geri was a wannabe IT girl!

formed a hatred for Izzy, which continued until just before she left the show, when they finally reconciled their differences. A brief dalliance with Lewis followed, but this soon fizzled out and it seemed as if Geri was never going to meet the man of her dreams.

It was on a holiday with her mother, the irrepressible Jacqui (Julie Peasgood), that Geri met and fell for the football ace, Jason Cunliffe. What followed was a tumultuous relationship as Geri had to cope with being the trophy and, at times, celebrity girlfriend and then, after Jason finally relented, she became the celebrity fiancée. This relationship reached a climax in the video, *Hollyoaks: Indecent Behaviour*, when Geri saw Jason's true colours as he was unfaithful to her and then turned a blind eye when his teammate, Scott, attempted to force himself on her. Geri was devastated that her fairy-tale prince had been exposed to be such a rogue. After much thought, she decided to go through with the wedding anyway and extract as much money as she could out of Jason — this was about revenge, not love.

It was this plan that led Geri to leave — she married Jason and then, as they left for a new life in Spain, threw him out of their limousine, informing him that their marriage was over and that she was going with her mother. As she left for the airport, Geri drove through Hollyoaks Village for one last time and bid a tearful farewell.

THE WRITING PROCESS

When *Hollyoaks* first began in 1995, it consisted of only three writers – creator and producer Phil Redmond, Roy Boulter and Andy Lynch. Andy and Roy had come across from Mersey Television's *Brookside*. Yet, as the show continued to grow in size, the writing team began slowly to expand to meet the increase in demand. *Hollyoaks* has always prided itself on producing great writers and has indeed proved itself to have a wealth of writing talent. *Hollyoaks* now has over sixteen writers, but the producers are still always on the look-out for fresh talent to add to the writing team.

Essential for any writer on the show to understand is the core of what makes *Hollyoaks* so different from its contemporaries – principally the ability to show life through the eyes of teenagers, without ever seeming patronizing or moralistic. Also important is that a writer understands the nature of the 'Hollyoaks spin'; *Hollyoaks* is unrivalled in its ability to juxtapose evenly balanced helpings of comedy and tragedy. Whilst most soaps tend to regard the comedy as peripheral, the producers of *Hollyoaks* view this as a central feature vital to the continuing success of the show. So whilst there will always be the Cindy, Luke and Lucy stories, the team endeavours to balance these in equal measures with the likes of Carol and the escapades of Max and O.B. One thing is certain; *Hollyoaks* will keep trying to come up with fresh and innovative storylines that encapsulate the lives of teenagers today. With the help of its team of brilliant writers, *Hollyoaks* will aim to constantly reinvent itself in order to remain as realistic and as necessary as it was back in 1995.

If a writer meets the *Hollyoaks* criteria, then they are invited to write a trial script for the show. If this is met with approval from the producers, they are held in consideration until there is a vacancy on the writing team.

MEET THE WRITERS: LUCY GOUGH

Lucy Gough has been with the show since its early days. Lucy wrote her first episode of *Hollyoaks* back in May 1996 and has remained with the show ever since. Lucy already had a flourishing career in writing prior to her appointment on the *Hollyoaks* team. She had written extensively for radio and theatre, and was short-listed for the BBC Wales Writer of the Year in 1994 for her play, *Crossing The Bar*. Lucy has played an important part in the show and has often retold her own life experiences through the lives of the characters in the show, most notably Cindy Cunningham.

How did you find out about *Hollyoaks*?

I had been writing for quite a few years for theatre and radio, particularly young people's theatre. I saw an article in the *Radio Times* about Phil Redmond and this new show he was doing called *Hollyoaks*. I remember

Lucy Gough

thinking that this was what television needed. I was really interested in it, so I applied and got an interview, and was asked to write half an episode. I remember my first storyline meeting when I suggested to Phil and Jo that they kill Kurt and bring him back as a ghost! I thought I was going to be sacked!

Can you remember your first episode?
I can remember a bit of it because Ollie and Stan were in it and Ollie was posting flowers to Susi Harrison through the letterbox. I also remember the sibling rivalry that was going on between Ollie and Kurt – that was very much part of the programme, with constant battles between the two boys. I used to love writing for Ollie because he was such a great character – he and Stan were a great pair and were lovely to write for.

What's a typical day for you?
I get up very early; walk the dog in the forest and then just work for the day. Occasionally I'll go out at lunchtime for another walk but I usually start early in the day and work through till the evening.

Why is Cindy's story personal to you?

I had my eldest son when I was in my teens. I left school at fifteen without any qualifications and then had my son a few years later. I think it's just a very distinctive experience having a child that young; it can happen to any girl and it's a story that needs telling. It has drama in it, but also there's the reality of having a child in your teens and that's what I found interesting with the Cindy story. There seems to be romanticism around it, but it's hard work, although I don't regret it for a single minute. The reality of not being able to go out with your mates every night and being woken up every two hours during the night and not knowing one end of a baby from another is the makings of some very rich drama. Having a baby when you're married or in your twenties or thirties is a very different experience. When you're just a kid yourself and you're looking at this *thing,* it's a different sort of story, and I was interested in following it through. It was Phil's idea that she didn't tell anyone she was pregnant and that was very hard to keep up, but worked very well. There was great poignancy in the fact that there was no one Cindy could turn to.

Do writers tend to use their own life experiences when developing stories for characters?

I think you do to a certain extent but you can't just write your own life all the time. You want to share those common experiences but you change them and twist them to accommodate the characters. You have to distil certain emotions but use them in a different way.

You've been writing for *Hollyoaks* for over six years. Which have been your most memorable characters and storylines?

I loved writing for Cindy, Stan and Ollie. I also enjoyed writing for Lewis and Tony. Now I really enjoy writing for Zara and Abby – I love those young, edgy characters. I also like the quirky characters like Jambo and Finn, the ones that come in with an off-the-wall philosophy to life. I think people like watching those characters. I think that that's what's required of a writer – to come in on things from a different perspective and make the audience look at things a different way for five minutes. I remember enjoying writing Kurt and Ruth's wedding and Cindy's sixteenth birthday, where she slept with Stan.

What makes *Hollyoaks* so successful?

I think that the show's success is the combination of quirkiness and drama. The show is often very brave, with stories such as the male rape and Lewis's suicide, yet is always ready to surprise with quirky comedy. The show has reinvented itself a couple of times over the years, not massively, but enough to keep it interesting and maintain its relevance.

What advice would you give to any budding writers?

Don't ever give up. You have to believe in yourself. You need to keep at it – keep writing, keep sending it out to people all the time. I remember sending one of my radio plays to someone and they sent it back to me and said it was extremely rude and they weren't going to touch it with a barge pole! I sent it to someone else – three days later he phoned and said he was doing it. You should try and get involved in whatever arts activities you can – creative writing classes, theatre workshops – and enter as many competitions as you can. The most important part is finding your own voice as a writer.

MEET THE WRITERS: NEIL JONES

Hollyoaks had always courted its fair share of controversy for its hard-hitting storylines. The episode that dealt with events leading up to Luke's rape is undoubtedly the episode that has attracted the most attention from audiences and critics alike. It is regarded as a significant benchmark for the show, yet as Neil Jones, the writer of this episode explains, the rape of Luke was never an attempt to grab the headlines. Rather, it seemed to be the most horrific climax possible to a long-running bullying storyline between Luke and Mark Gibbs.

> We never actually sat down at a storyline meeting and decided to do an episode about a male rape. The story we wanted to tell was about a young man who seemed to have it all being driven to the brink of suicide by bullying. The rape element only appeared when we were trying to hit on something which Luke would feel he could not recover from. I think because it evolved naturally like this we avoided accusations of being sensationalist. But once we had decided to take on the issue, we knew that the episode would attract a lot of attention and reach viewers who had maybe never seen the show before, so I was really conscious of wanting to make this the best *Hollyoaks* script I had written.

One part of this storyline that struck a major chord with the audience was the painful journey Luke went through as he tried to come to terms with what had happened to him. It took him over two months to tell his brother, Adam, and this was only after Luke had tried to drive his car into a wall in a desperate attempt to kill himself. The audience was behind Luke at every stage of his struggle as he tried to tell his parents, and ultimately felt his pain and frustration when he couldn't go through with it. The story was a slow-burner, yet exemplified *Hollyoaks*'s wish never to sensationalize a story. We travelled along at Luke's pace, knowing that it would be a long time before Luke achieved any sort of closure or acceptance of what had happened to him.

With a story as delicate as male rape, the writers, producers and script department work closely with the *Hollyoaks* researcher, who tries to make sure that story is depicted as realistically as possible. The researcher spoke to several victims of male rape, rape counsellors and examined countless case studies. It was evident from the research taken that male rape was regarded as an 'unmentionable' crime, which gave the producers of the show even more impetus to make sure that they acted as a voice to those victims too frightened and too ashamed to admit what happened to them. As Neil explained:

> We wanted to get across that male rape is nothing to do with sexuality but with brutality and humiliation – and that it often goes unreported. One reaction which recurred a lot during the making of the episode was from men saying there was no way 'that' would ever happen to them. It made me realize that this was something which needed to be brought out into the open, but I wasn't certain we'd got it right until we received letters and emails from people who had been through similar experiences, telling us they were pleased that we had tackled it.

MEET THE WRITERS: KADDY BENYON

One essential element that enables *Hollyoaks* to retain its freshness of approach and vitality is to make sure that the show has a constant intake of young writers, who are able to inject a new level of energy into the show. One such writer

Kaddy Benyon

DID YOU KNOW...?

Roy Boulter who wrote for the show until 1997, used to be a drummer for indie band, The Farm.

is Kaddy Benyon. At twenty-eight, Kaddy is one of the youngest writers on the show. She began as a script assistant on the show back in 1995 and, after several years in the script department, she went on to be a storyliner for Channel 5's *Family Affairs*. Kaddy returned to *Hollyoaks* as a writer in May 1999 and has been with the show ever since. As well as writing for the show, Kaddy wrote the novel, *Luke's Secret Diary,* which sold nearly 50,000 copies.

How do you create a new character on the show?
With new characters I tend to look at who's in the show already and see if there's any gaps where there's a *type* of character missing. Then I look at famous people in the teen magazines – popstars and people like that and steal bits of their characters. Then I usually add a bit about people I know if I think there's an interesting facet to their personality, and then I send the suggestions in to the producers and they decide if they like them or not.

Tell me about a character you have created.
I created the character of Becca Hayton. With Becca, I thought it would be quite interesting to bring someone in who had been quite spoiled, who was quite naïve, had been pampered and is a bit of a princess. I wanted to see her getting used to student life and living with other people, and how she would adapt to those kind of circumstances. Becca was also incredibly naïve with men and I thought it was interesting to see her used and abused, and learning from her mistakes.

Which storylines have you enjoyed writing the most?
I tend to enjoy writing for the younger characters because I'm naturally drawn to school-age type stories. Friendships between girls are a big thing for me, falling in and falling out of favour, bullying, that type of thing. I generally like the quirky characters. I used to love writing for Carol because she always saw things from a different angle.

What makes *Hollyoaks* stand out?
It's the only show that has a real sense of humour and I think we are quirky and we're proud of that. Even though our characters look gorgeous, like Mandy, we often make them self-deprecating and that makes them more likeable for the audience.

What advice would you give to budding young writers?
Don't give up because you *will* get knock-backs. I think the test of a true writer is to keep going – if you've got a dream, pursue it, because people respect you for that. Keep writing and keep practising – write every day, even if it's just a diary – write what you know and read anything you can.

HOW A STORY EVOLVES

The journey a story goes on from its humble beginnings in the minds of the producers and writers, through to its arrival on our screens, is a long and drawn-out one, where the story will be scrutinized, altered and built upon to fit into the lives of our characters. For example, if a writer came up with an idea of dealing with the subject of diabetes, the team of writers and producers discuss the idea, deciding if it has enough weight and sufficient credibility to become a long-running storyline. They then talk about which possible characters the storyline could be appropriate for, and what impact it would have on their lives. If the writers and producers are in agreement, they decide on a time at which to start the story and then begin to evaluate the directions in which it could take the show and the character. The researcher would then become involved to ensure that the writers and producers have the necessary research to create an accurate story. For a story such as diabetes, they would endeavour to speak to as many diabetics and doctors as possible, so that they can guarantee that the story is authentic.

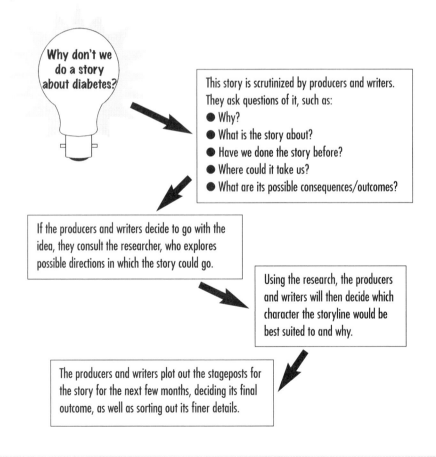

Why don't we do a story about diabetes?

This story is scrutinized by producers and writers. They ask questions of it, such as:
- Why?
- What is the story about?
- Have we done the story before?
- Where could it take us?
- What are its possible consequences/outcomes?

If the producers and writers decide to go with the idea, they consult the researcher, who explores possible directions in which the story could go.

Using the research, the producers and writers will then decide which character the storyline would be best suited to and why.

The producers and writers plot out the stageposts for the story for the next few months, deciding its final outcome, as well as sorting out its finer details.

THE SCRIPT DEPARTMENT

At the heart of *Hollyoaks* is the script department which has seen expansion and growth like no other department. It began with just a script associate and a script assistant to deal with scripts for the once-weekly show. It currently consists of three script associates, four script assistants, a script supervisor, a script secretary, three producers, a line producer and a series producer! Not only does the script department have the task of producing four scripts a week, it also has to produce storylines every two weeks which detail what will be happening in six months' time in *Hollyoaks*!

Confused? Then the following chart might help you to understand the complicated workings of the *Hollyoaks* script department!

STORYLINE MEETING

The series producer, producers, writers and script department discuss possible storylines.

The script department writes up the storylines and then distributes scripts to all heads of department and writers.

The producers decide which writer will write each particular episode.

PRE-COMMISSIONING MEETING

The producers and heads of department meet to discuss the storylines.

COMMISSIONING MEETING

The producers and writers discuss storylines before the writers begin work on their scripts.

The writers deliver the first drafts of their scripts. These are read by producers and script associates, and notes are given back to writers.

The writers deliver the second draft of their scripts. These are read again by producers and script associates and more notes are given back to the writers.

The writers deliver their third and final drafts. After the script has been checked, it is given to the director assigned to the episode to read.

WRITER/DIRECTOR MEETING

The director, writer and producer have a meeting to discuss the script. This is an opportunity for the director to offer any suggestions for the script.

The writer will incorporate the changes to the script suggested by the director and producer from the writer/director meeting to produce the final draft of the script.

The script department proofread the script to check for errors, and then the scripts are printed and distributed to the whole production team.

The script is now ready to go into production. The actors finally get their scripts and the cameras start rolling.

BEN DAVIES *played by Marcus Patric*

Firefighter Ben Davies first appeared on our screens in August 2000, and almost instantly fell for Cindy Cunningham. This relationship marked Cindy's departure, as, struggling to prevent her daughter from being taken away by Social Services, she fled the country. Ben soon turned his attentions to Mandy, even though he knew Luke wanted her back. Despite his affair with Mandy, Ben proved to be a vital friend to Luke, helping him get over his rape ordeal. However, when Luke found out about Mandy and Ben, he felt devastated and betrayed, leaving the guilty pair to reconsider their future together. Ben soon grew tired of Mandy's impetuous behaviour and reverted to being a 'lad about town'. He continues to have the odd dalliance with the likes of Ellie and Izzy, but seems perfectly content just to have a good time with the lads, whilst trying to keep his wayward sister, Abby, under control.

Name: Marcus Patric

Age: 22

Place of Birth: Portsmouth

Earliest Memory: Watching Liverpool thrash Pompey at Fratton Park – 4-1

Favourite Film: *Boyz N the Hood*

Favourite Band: Varied music taste – maybe Coldplay

Ideal Woman: Carmen Electra!

Favourite holiday destination: Brazil

What three things would you take with you to a desert island: A football, a blow-up woman and some eggs

What were you doing before *Hollyoaks*?

I was travelling for just under six months in Brazil; I went there with a couple of mates I was working with in London, who were Brazilian. I was spending the money that I'd earned from my couple of years working as a model and as a barman. I just wanted to get out and do something, and when you're doing that kind of work, it allows you to do that. I wouldn't have been able to do that now, so I'm just glad to have got it out of my system. I just went over there, came back with no money and wondered what I could do. Then I heard about *On the Pull*.

Tell me about *On the Pull.*

I heard about it on the radio and thought that I might as well go along. I've always loved acting and that's what I always wanted to do, I just never thought I'd get the chance. I went up to London the next day and saw the queues as soon as I got out of the train station; I think there were about 20,000 people at the auditions. I was a bit late, so I was right at the back. Eventually, I got in and just got through stage after stage and then a hundred of us got asked to come back the next day. I went to that, got through again and then they phoned me the next day and asked me to go to a final audition up in Liverpool. The more it looked like I might have a chance, the more nervous I got. Somehow I got through and ended up getting a part!

You started in the show almost immediately – were you nervous?

When I got the part, they told me that I was starting in about three days' time! They said that I'd be seeing Cindy and it was a storyline with the baby. It threw me in at the deep end and I was glad of that – I was awful at first and then got a bit better.

After a while, we brought in your dad and your sister. Do you enjoy working as part of a family?

I love the family that we've got. Although there's just three of us, people say to me that it looks like a really solid, friendly

family. You've got the Morgans, who are going through awful troubles; you've got the Cunninghams, who are at each other's throats and one of their sons has just died. The Davies are the only family with silly little problems; Abby's getting upset about Lee and more importantly, it looks real and we all get on really well together.

You've had your fair share of comedy recently. Do you prefer comedy or drama?

Ever since the video [*Hollyoaks: Indecent Behaviour*] they've [the writers] been giving me more and more comedy to do. Before that, I used to get the same kind of stuff as Gary [Luke] and it was on more of a serious note, but I do like doing the odd bit of comedy. The Ben and Izzy storyline in the video was a turning point for Ben and me; I think it brought something out of me that I hadn't showed before. Maybe I wasn't that comfortable before, but ever since the video I've been more comfortable playing Ben. I think I understand him better.

What direction would you like Ben to go in?

I'd like him to get a girlfriend, but then again, I love him being the ladies' man that he is. Ben's always been a bit of a loveable rogue and I like that. He needs a mate and he needs a girlfriend, but other than that I'm really happy with him!

FINN, JANUARY 2002

Played by James Redmond
June 1998–January 2002

When Tony discovered the supposed vagrant sleeping in Jambo's old shed, little did he realize that this philosophical, free-spirited charmer would become one of his closest friends. Immediately, Tony went on a mission to have Finn evicted from the shed, beginning a comical rivalry that would continue throughout Finn's time in Chester. Finn's father was in prison and his mother was dead, so he tended to drift from place to place – he had no idea how long he would remain in Chester, yet he planned to stick around and see what opportunities came his way.

Whilst persevering in his war with Tony, Finn soon hooked up with Lewis and together they ran a market in the Yard, with Finn specializing in selling antiques. Along the way, Finn embarked on quite a few money-making ventures, the most infamous being the time he decided to use his double-decker bus as a tour bus around Chester, procuring the services of Carol as the unsuspecting tour guide. Finn's enigmatic status attracted considerable interest from the women in Chester – Jude, Kate, Carol and Geri, even more

First seen: Crashed out in Jambo's shed, instantly incurring the wrath of Tony!

Last seen: On board a barge sailing off into the sunset with a mystery woman

Finest moment: Taking revenge on Lewis for his attack on Ruth and, later, taking the sick Lewis to hospital

Worst moment: When Victoria ended their marriage

Funniest moment: When he unwittingly killed Carol's dog Meryl and then dyed another poodle black to try to fool her

Love of his life: Victoria, however he only realized this after losing her

Most embarrassing moment: In Barcelona, when Tony shot him in the backside with a harpoon gun!

Most likely to say: Something to annoy Tony, a theme that would be constant throughout his time on the show

Least likely to say: 'That doesn't sound very practical.' Finn never embraced convention and would tackle anything, however extraordinary.

Place most likely to have been seen: Anywhere in the vicinity of the Yard – he liked to remain at the heart of his empire

Hobbies/Interests: Antiques, the unconventional, and money-making schemes

so when he revealed that he was, in fact, Lord Kildiggin and heir to a castle in Ireland! True to his nature, Finn declined the inheritance of his castle and although he retained his title, he preferred the life of an anonymous drifter.

Carol and Finn embarked on a passionate and sometimes tumultuous relationship, climaxing in a marathon 48-hour session on Finn's bus, yet his free-spirited nature and roving eye brought the relationship to a premature close. Finn and Lewis soon found another money-spinning idea when they began to organize Nineties revival nights at a local club, giving them the idea of building their own nightclub. After using Finn's title to secure a bank loan, they finally got the go-ahead to build The Loft. Problems in Finn's relationship with Tony resurfaced when an unsuspecting Finn embarked on an affair with Victoria (Fiona Mollison). Even Finn was shocked to discover that she was Tony's mother! Unsurprisingly, Tony was actively against the union, but the two carried on regardless. Soon Victoria became Victoria Finnigan and along with the marriage came Finn's new role – as Tony's stepfather!

Finn and Victoria's marriage lasted only six months, collapsing after Victoria discovered that Finn had been unfaithful. The end of his marriage marked the beginning of Finn's life crisis, when he began to question what it was he wanted from life. Whilst business at The Loft continued to thrive, Finn was becoming increasingly bored with life and, after learning that Lewis had got himself into debt and had put the future of the club in jeopardy, he persuaded

Tony to buy Lewis out. Finn returned the favour by buying into Tony's new restaurant and they both became embroiled in a new set of adventures in *Hollyoaks: Movin' On*. Finn's life crisis continued, however, and Lewis's shocking death only underlined his belief that life was indeed too short.

Whilst Finn returned to *Hollyoaks,* it wasn't long before he moved on. He left the running of The Loft to Tony, saying that he wanted to return to the life he used to have – the life of a drifter and, more importantly, a life of uncertainty. And so Finn boarded a barge with a mystery woman and sailed off into the sunset... and *Hollyoaks* bid farewell to one of its most eccentric, yet ultimately most endearing characters.

IZZY CORNWELL *played by Elize du Toit*

Izzy Cornwell arrived on our screens in September 2000, when Adam Morgan saved her from drowning in the college pool. Izzy left a strong impression on both Adam and the audience – she was strong-willed, feisty and continually saying the wrong thing. Adam soon fell for Izzy and abandoned Geri for her. Thus began a war of words between Geri and Izzy, which continued for over a year, climaxing in their one-to-one combat in Game 4 IT, when Geri managed to beat Izzy. Izzy has been eternally unlucky in love – she split up with Adam when she found out that he had been videoing the house for a film project; had a brief dalliance with Dan but this didn't work out, and resigned herself to remaining single. Izzy is certainly no one's fool and proved this in no uncertain terms when she taught Ben Davies a lesson on the back of the bus in the video Hollyoaks: Indecent Behaviour. *Izzy's version of her harmonious home life was brought into dispute when her mother, Patty, arrived and soon hooked up with Jack Osborne, exposing Izzy's parents' marriage as a sham. Izzy has now found happiness in Tony, although there is a constant spark with Ben... Is there more to this than meets the eye?*

Name: Elize du Toit

Age: 22

Place of Birth: Grahamstown, South Africa

Earliest Memory: Brother slamming a door on my pinkie finger and the nail falling off

Favourite Film: *True Romance*

Favourite Band: The Supremes

Ideal Man: Maximus (the character, not Russell Crowe) from Gladiator

Favourite holiday destination: South Africa

Who would you want to play you in a film of your life: Sarah Jessica Parker and Cameron Diaz blend

What three things would you take with you to a desert island: Designer sunglasses, a sexy man and my piano

What were you doing before *Hollyoaks*?
I was doing a History degree at Edinburgh University; I'd done two years out of a four-year course.

What made you decide to apply to *On the Pull*?
My boyfriend at the time told me about the audition and we'd just got back from holiday. I was in London at the time but when we returned to Edinburgh, I found out they were auditioning there as well, so I went along.

Tell me about your audition.
I went quite early and queued up for a couple of hours. The first stage of the

audition was in front of Dorothy Andrew and you had to stand in front her of and say a few words about yourself and then they go 'yes' or 'no'. They said 'no, thanks' and sent me away. My friend was behind me in the queue, and while they were doing him, someone said to me, 'Actually can you go to that room', so I almost didn't get through the first stage! The next day was the second round of auditions, where the numbers had been whittled down to about fifty people, and then we actually read scripts, and then the group got whittled down even further to about fifteen people. We were asked to come back the next day and then after that I waited for about three weeks and then I got a call to tell me that I was one of the last set of people and the auditions were going to be held in Liverpool in front of Series Producer Jo Hallows and Executive Producer Phil Redmond. It was an all-day audition. It was exhausting and throughout the day they decreased numbers until we [Elize, Marcus, Andrew and Lesley] were told we had the parts.

Can you still remember your first day on set?
My first scene was in the college pool; it was awful because I had to be in a bikini – every girl's worst nightmare – being in a bikini on national television! I think I was quite nervous because when I look back at the episode, I looked really nervous. It was fun, though, I was working with David Brown [Adam] and I remember Tim Downie [Sam] and David Andrews the Director.

What's been your favourite memory so far of being in *Hollyoaks*?
I really enjoyed doing the video [*Hollyoaks: Indecent Behaviour*] because it was nice working on a different project and it was fun. David Richardson was fantastic and I had quite a fun little storyline with Marcus and that's probably been my favourite episode so far.

Who do you think Izzy would be best suited to?
I think the natural way for it to go is with Ben Davies, because of what was started in the video – it worked well between us and was fun to watch.

HOLLYOAKS ALUMNI

BAZZ – TOBY SAWYER
Recent credits include Tom in ITV1's *Crossroads* and Louis in the acclaimed film *Quills*

CAROL –
NATALIE CASEY
Last seen playing Donna in BBC2's *Two Pints of lager (And a Packet of Crisps)* opposite Will Mellor, and is a regular host on MTV

CINDY – STEPHANIE WARING
Last seen playing Tina in Sky One's *Crash Palace* and can be seen later in 2002 as Ricky Tomlinson's daughter in BBC1's *Nice Guy Eddie*

DARREN – ASHLEY TAYLOR DAWSON
Can be seen as Ashley in *StarStreet* as well as himself in the hit band Allstars!

GERI –
JOANNA TAYLOR
Soon to be seen as WPC Jackie Brown in BBC1's *Mersey Beat*

JAMBO –
WILL MELLOR
Can be seen playing Jack in BBC1's *Casualty* and Gaz in BBC2's *Two Pints of lager (And a Packet of Crisps)*

JASMINE – ELLY FAIRMAN
Recent credits include Lucy in the film *Small Time Obsession*

JUDE –
DAVINIA TAYLOR
Last seen playing Alison in Sky One's *Is Harry On The Boat?* (also featuring Will Mellor as Greg)

KURT –
JEREMY EDWARDS
Can be seen playing Danny in BBC1's *Holby City*

LEWIS – BEN HULL
Can be seen playing Dr Gary Parr in Channel 4's *Brookside*

LUCY – KERRIE TAYLOR
Recent credits include Beth in ITV1's *Where The Heart Is* and Meg in BBC1's *Clocking Off 2*

LUKE –
GARY LUCY
Recent credits include Kyle Pascoe in ITV1's *Footballers Wives*

MADDIE – YASMIN BANNERMAN
Recent credits include Melinda in *Maybe Baby*, Jessica in ITV1's *Cold Feet* and Vanessa in BBC1's *Happy Birthday Shakespeare*

NATASHA –
SHEBAH RONAY
Is now a film critic for the *News of the World!*

ROB – WARREN DEROSA
Last seen playing John in Sky One's *Crash Palace* opposite Stephanie Waring

So you think you know everything there is to know about *Hollyoaks*? Well, here's a list of questions that even the most die-hard fan would struggle to answer. See how many you manage to get right.

1 Carol Groves has a sister. What's her name and where does she work?

2 What was the name of Jambo's dog?

3 Ruth Osborne lost a relative in the first year of *Hollyoaks*. Who was this and how did they die?

4 What was Finn's full name?

5 What was the name of the band that featured Lucy Benson, Carol Groves, Bazz and Lewis Richardson?

6 How many children does Jack Osborne have?

7 Who was Margaret?

8 Why was Geri arrested?

9 Ben had to rescue Tony from a car because he had a what up his trousers?

10 What was the secret that Stan took to his grave?

11 What invention did Jambo test at Kurt and Ollie Benson's 1995 Christmas party?

12 What was the name of Carol's dog that met with an unfortunate end?

13 What was the name of Sol and Gina's *real* mother and how did she die?

14 What was the name of Tony's restaurant in *Hollyoaks: Movin' On*?

15 What football team do Brian and Mr Morgan both support?

16 When Beth first came onto the show, she discovered that she had a rare literary talent. What was it?

17 What was the name of the bike instructor who tempted Julie away from Tony?

18 When the show first began, who was Ollie's girlfriend?

19 What is O.B.'s real name?

20 Jambo had a half-brother and half-sister – what were their names?

21 What was the play that Max and O.B. appeared in?

22 What was Kurt's affectionate term for the thing that woke him up at 6.59 every morning?

23 Who was Mandy Richardson's first boyfriend?

24 What was the name of the business guru whom Tony blamed for ruining his video shop?

25 Max, O.B. and Mr C made a record. What was it called?

26 What was the name of Tony's video shop?

27 Where did Helen give birth to baby Tom and who delivered the baby?

28 Who did Tony find in his bed when the gang went to Ireland?

29 Who was Beth Morgan briefly engaged to?

30 Why did Zara have to go and see a psychiatrist?

31 Who stood against Mr C and Tony in the local elections?

32 Who was Luke's first sexual conquest when he arrived in Chester?

33 How and where did Dawn die?

34 Who was Jude's partner in crime?

35 Assistant caretaker Wayne has a pet rat. What was it called?

36 What was the name of Jack Osborne's first wife?

37 What's the name of Alex's robot?

38 What job did Carol leave to do?

39 Matt was due to go skiing with Geri and the rest of the gang. Why couldn't he go?

40 What was the name of Izzy's first boyfriend?

ANSWERS

1. Anita, Chester Zoo.
2. Deefer.
3. Natasha – her drink was spiked with drugs.
4. Rory Finnigan.
5. The Crazy Bazz Studs.
6. Three – Ruth, Darren and Bethany (Dawn's daughter).
7. Jambo's fibreglass cow.
8. For begging.
9. A snake.
10. That Cindy was pregnant with his child.
11. The snogging helmet.
12. Meryl.
13. Louise – she committed suicide.
14. Gnosh.
15. Cowdenbeath – 'the blue Brazil'!
16. Poetry writing.
17. Bruce.
18. Julie Matthews.
19. Sam O'Brien.
20. Jake and Emily.
21. *The Changeling.*
22. 'The Unidentified Bleeping Object'.
23. Ollie Benson.
24. Hank P. Ackerman.
25. 'Get Down With That Thing'.
26. Got it Taped.
27. In the back of her car – Mandy.
28. Finn's dead gran!
29. Rob Hawthorne.
30. She burnt down the school art block.
31. Matt, representing the Party Party!
32. Ruth Osborne.
33. Leukaemia, in a rowing boat with Jambo.
34. Benny.
35. Thornley.
36. Celia.
37. Phat.
38. Singing on a cruise ship.
39. He broke his leg on a dry-ski slope.
40. Eric.

HOLLYOAKS: LUKE'S SECRET DIARY

After 15 March 2000, Luke will never be the same again. Containing his intimate thoughts as he progresses from cocky wide-boy and star of the football field to rape victim, this is Luke's story in his own words.
ISBN 0 7522 7210 1 £3.99

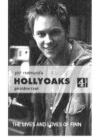

HOLLYOAKS: THE LIVES AND LOVES OF FINN

Who is Finn: a convict's son? A man who would sleep with his mate's mum? Someone who'd cheat on his girlfriend? Or is he all of these...? This is the inside story of one of *Hollyoaks* most popular characters.
ISBN 0 7522 7211 X £3.99

HOLLYOAKS: STOLEN E-MAILS

When personal e-mails turn up in the wrong inboxes, suspicion grips Hollyoaks. Who is stirring up trouble by redirecting mail? Accusations fly but all the while the mystery hacker is uncovering secrets that could tear people's lives apart...
ISBN 0 7522 1955 3 £4.99

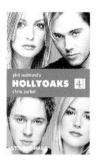

HOLLYOAKS: LUKE'S JOURNAL:
A NEW BEGINNING

In this sequel to *Luke's Secret Diary* Luke is trying to pick up the pieces after the rape. But when the trial causes terrible repercussions for the Morgans, and Mandy wants to be just friends, he realises leaving the past behind him isn't that easy...
ISBN 0 7522 1954 5 £4.99

HOLLYOAKS: RUNNING WILD

You're seventeen, strong-willed and sassy. You're on holiday in Ibiza having the time of your life, when suddenly it occurs to you – why go home? In *Running Wild*, Ellie reveals all about her life abroad, while Dan, Gary and Toby reveal what happened to those she left behind.
ISBN 07522 6474 5 £4.99

HOLLYOAKS: SEEING RED

When her sister Ellie disappeared while on holiday, Lisa's life was torn apart. Frustrated and lonely, the only way she could find release was to turn against herself. *Seeing Red* tells the story of Lisa's struggle to understand how her life spiralled out of control.
ISBN 07522 6475 3 £4.99

You can order copies direct from the Channel 4 Shop by calling 0870 1234 344.